Human Design for Business

HUMAN DESIGN
for Business

Discover Your Unique Blueprint to Build a Business and Life You Love

JAMIE L. PALMER

NEW YORK

LONDON • NASHVILLE • MELBOURNE • VANCOUVER

Human Design for Business

Discover Your Unique Blueprint to Build a Business and Life You Love

Published in New York, New York, by Morgan James Publishing. Morgan James is a trademark of Morgan James, LLC. www.MorganJamesPublishing.com

Proudly distributed by Publishers Group West®

A **FREE** ebook edition is available for you
or a friend with the purchase of this print book.

_____

CLEARLY SIGN YOUR NAME ABOVE

Instructions to claim your free ebook edition:
1. Visit MorganJamesBOGO.com
2. Sign your name CLEARLY in the space above
3. Complete the form and submit a photo
   of this entire page
4. You or your friend can download the ebook
   to your preferred device

ISBN 9781636981680 paperback
ISBN 9781636981697 ebook
Library of Congress Control Number:
2023933657

Morgan James is a proud partner of Habitat for Humanity Peninsula
and Greater Williamsburg. Partners in building since 2006.

Get involved today! Visit: www.morgan-james-publishing.com/giving-back

DEDICATION

I could not have written this book without the love and relentless support of the following people:

To my husband, thank you for always believing in me and for loving me exactly as I am. I wouldn't be who I am today without you. I love you with every fiber of my being.

To my kids, you are my universe. I am so grateful you chose me as your mom. You both have taught me so much, and I've grown so much because of how you move into the world. I love you.

To my dear Helen, there are no words yet so many words. Thank you for seeing me, recognizing me, and empowering me to own my voice, my power, and my magic. This book would not be here today if it weren't for your 6/2 MG magic.

CONTENTS

INTRODUCTION

I wouldn't say I chose Human Design. It chose me. I stumbled across Human Design thanks to the Instagram algorithm and learned I was Projector. At the time, I was quite miserable, straddling two worlds: running my social media agency and trying to grow my Business Ecosystem Builder group coaching program. I was burned out and bitter in true Projector fashion. I felt like I was going through the motions of life but not really living it. I had spent the vast majority of the last year knowing I didn't want to do social media anymore, but I never had 100 percent certainty that is was the right decision or any idea of what to do next. Then I discovered I was an emotional authority, which meant I would never have 100 percent certainty on any of my decisions in life—70–80 percent was a yes for me. That was the aha moment I needed to make a change.

The more I dug into Human Design, the more sense it made to me. I couldn't unsee it. Many of the ups and downs I had experienced over the years began to make so much sense through the lens of Human Design. I dug deeper and deeper and studied everything I could get my hands on. I shared it with family, then friends, then clients. I began to see themes in business with every aspect of the Human Design chart.

As I gained more experience in supporting clients with their business while using their Human Design chart, clients began to get better, more predictable results with more ease because I could name what might come up along the way.

I wove together vibrant threads for different aspects of business, and this book alongside the HD Your Biz program was born. The first launch of the HD Your Biz beta program defied all the odds of a launch, with fifty-seven incredible souls enrolling from a list built entirely on my social media agency. My goal was five. I was blown away. What was even wilder was that nearly 90 percent of the students who enrolled finished the thirteen-week program. Launch strategists that I speak with still can't believe I was able to do this. I attribute it to the fact that I committed to being in my Projector self.

Human Design is a tool you can use to better understand yourself so that you can create more ease and flow in your life. When integrated with business, it makes running a business happen with more congruence to who you are and how you are designed to operate in the world.

I wrote this book because I believe that if each one of us could be more of who we are, the world would be a better place. I've supported entrepreneurs and small business owners my entire career. Entrepreneurs are people who want to make an impact in the world, to create change, to disrupt. They are people who give up perfectly good jobs to pursue something more, to create a ripple effect with their work. I believe my role is to be a steward of how to create a life and business on your terms in congruence with who you are meant to be. When you can do this with more ease and flow, you attract more abundance, make a bigger impact, and fall in love with your life (and business) again.

I hope this book meets you where you are and supports you in gaining more understanding of who you are. I hope you give yourself grace and compassion for the missteps you may have taken along the way. I hope you use this tool to better understand yourself, make more congruent decisions in your business, and find more joy, abundance, and flow in every aspect of your business and life.

HOW TO MAKE THE MOST OF THIS BOOK

This book is divided into two parts. The first part is centered around helping you deepen your understanding of your Human Design. The second part is designed to give you an understanding of how to use your Human Design in business.

I first recommend you print out your Human Design chart, and you can do so on my website: https://www.jamielpalmer.com/download-your-human-design-chart/

Then I recommend going though part 1 of the book and reading the sections that are present in your chart. You can dive into your type, profile, centers, and authority. Read each section that applies to your chart. This will support you in gaining a better understanding of who you are and your design, with recommendations in each section.

For part 2 of the book, I recommend reading it from start to finish. This will give you a better understanding of how to leverage your design at a high level for your business model, sales and marketing, offers and systems, and productivity.

HD YOUR BIZ

*We are told to let our light shine, and if it does, we won't need
to tell anybody it does. Lighthouses don't fire cannons
to call attention to their shining—they just shine.*
—Dwight L. Moody

When I think about Human Design, I love thinking about a lighthouse. Your own unique blueprint is sort of like your lighthouse. You can use this lighthouse to get you back home to who you are again and again. Its light shines brightly on the sea during a clear night, and it pierces through the fog during stormy days.

It's a guide to help you find your way back home again to who you were truly born to be.

But the reality is, on the journey through life, we can get pulled out to sea by the undertow, we can lose sight of the shore, we can end up in new lands, and we can get jostled about by waves.

All of this pulls us further and further away from who we are truly meant to be. We end up in a foreign place wondering how we got there.

Until one day we wake up—usually when we've been hit with a storm or we've stopped ignoring that inner tug and longing, or both—realizing we've lost sight of our light. We end up in a place many miles from where we intended, and we feel this ache to go back home again.

While the fog might make it hard for us to navigate the water or while the storms may come and go, when we can find our beacon of light—our light-house—we will always know our way back home again, bringing something new back with us.

It is in this coming and going that we uncover more about ourselves. Our lights shine brighter and brighter. It becomes easier to navigate your way back home again because you know the way. Even on the darkest nights, you can find your way back to your beacon, your lighthouse.

We are here to explore, go on adventures, and embrace freedom while simultaneously coming back home again. Each adventure uncovers a new piece of us. Each homecoming renews our sense of individuality. Each exploration is another confirmation of who we are. And the freedom . . . it shows us we are each part of a bigger whole.

Download the Human Design For Business Workbook to support you on your journey. www.humandesignforbusinessbook.com

THE HIERARCHY OF THE HUMAN DESIGN CHART

When I first started learning about Human Design, created by Ra Uru Hu in 1992, I wish someone had actually taken the time to explain to me the depth of the system. It can be a great source of understanding for each of us. It is built layer upon layer while always anchoring back into your strategy and authority.

Here is a visual of different layers within the chart and the process that they are built upon. In Human Design, we always anchor back into your strategy and authority. From there, the layers build the type, profile, centers, circuits, gates and channels, definitions, environment, and then the incarnation cross as the top, sort of like a compass to direct you toward your purpose in life.

Most of what is shared in Human Design has a duality to it—a stark contrast or a polarization. For example, the not-self and the signature themes. The defined and undefined centers. It is in this duality that we find meaning and make sense of ourselves and our place in the world. We get a true understanding of who we are. Embracing this duality is a big part of living in congruence with your design.

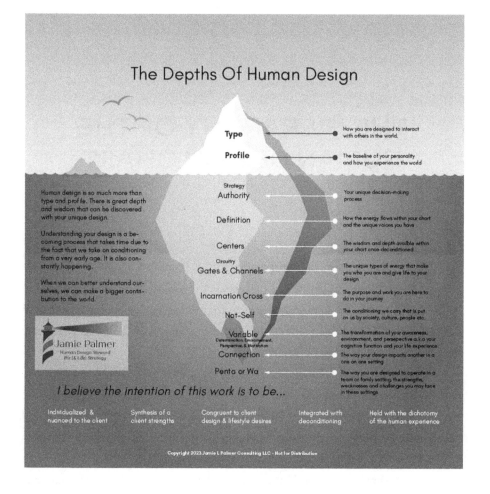

The Depths Of Human Design

Type — How you are designed to interact with others in the world.

Profile — The baseline of your personality and how you experience the world

Human design is so much more than type and profile. There is great depth and wisdom that can be discovered with your unique design.

Understanding your design is a becoming process that takes time due to the fact that we take on conditioning from a very early age. It is also constantly happening.

When we can better understand ourselves, we can make a bigger contribution to the world.

Strategy
Authority — Your unique decision-making process

Definition — How the energy flows within your chart and the unique voices you have

Centers — The wisdom and depth available within your chart once deconditioned

Circuitry
Gates & Channels — The unique types of energy that make you who you are and give life to your design

Incarnation Cross — The purpose and work you are here to do in your journey

Not-Self — The conditioning we carry that is put on us by society, culture, people etc.

Variable
Determination, Environment, Perspective, & Motivation — The transformation of your awareness, environment, and perspective a.k.a your cognitive function and your life experience

Connection — The way your design impacts another in a one on one setting

Penta or Wa — The way you are designed to operate in a team or family setting, the strengths, weaknesses and challenges you may face in these settings

Jamie Palmer
Human Design Steward
Biz (& Life) Strategy

I believe the intention of this work is to be...

Individualized & nuanced to the client

Synthesis of a client strengths

Congruent to client design & lifestyle desires

Integrated with deconditioning

Held with the dichotomy of the human experience

Part 1—
Human Design

What Does It Mean to Be a Projector?

You are a magnetic, insightful guide for those who invite you into their world. Your recognition comes when you explore your passion and wait for the invitation before offering up your wisdom. Your brilliance is a gift to this world; save it for those who are eager to hear it. Rest easy knowing you are magnetic. Step into your power. Believe it.

THE PROJECTOR EXPERIENCE

P rojectors are not here to redefine what it means to work. In fact, Projectors are here to guide, not do, literally. Projectors are not designed to be in the doing. Wild but it's true. Projectors are the leaders of our future. When following their strategy and authority, Projectors are here to guide the other types in order to help them live in congruence with their design and fulfill their purpose.

The Projector is often conditioned from a very early age to believe that they are a Generator, and that they "should" be doing, responding, and taking action. Often, if you go to an event, the Projector is the busiest person in the room. Running around doing all of the things. When, in fact, it would be more congruent for a healthy Projector to be resting and pursuing their passions while they wait for the invitation to guide people or the recognition for having guided people.

Everything in our modern society is built for Generators, so it is no surprise that most Projectors are conditioned to believe they are Generators.

Often this leads to the not-self theme for the Projector of bitterness and resentment.

A great example of this is when a Projector gives advice without first being invited or recognized. The Projector offers up great advice they know will support the other person; however, the other person wasn't ready or open to hearing the advice, so they went and did what they wanted to do anyway. They chose to ignore the Projector's guidance, leaving the Projector feeling bitter that the person didn't listen to what they had to say.

Most Projectors can think of one or two or maybe ten examples of this in their lives. For me, when I've given advice without the invitation, especially in business, it often appears as this nagging feeling of everything on paper looks right but something is off. It is often hard to put a finger on what exactly it is, but you can feel it's not right.

Alternatively, Projectors can think of a time when they had a great experience with a client or a person in their life. Energetically, they felt seen and heard. They watched someone else thrive, and they knew that it was as a result of their guidance and wisdom. That is an example of a Projector being in congruence with their strategy.

The challenge of being a Projector is learning the signals that their bodies send to tell them to stop. Since Projectors have an undefined sacral, they can often struggle to know when it is time to switch gears or stop. Think of it like a broken light switch stuck in the on position. Projectors struggle to know when enough is enough (since we are living in a Generator world) and will push themselves past their body's breaking point.

Most Projectors have struggled or will struggle with burnout at some point since they are conditioned from childhood to behave like Generators—to keep going, going, going. Honoring and listening to their body's cues as to when it is time to stop is important to living their strategy. This may mean setting clear boundaries around work, stopping before they are exhausted, going to bed before they are tired, and working less. Remember, Projectors are here to guide, not do.

When a Projector is in their signature goal, success will flow to them with ease. Invitations will be abundant, and the Projector will use their guiding energy for others creating success in their lives. It is this success after success that will fuel them and keep them out of their not-self of bitterness and resentment. It is in this success that Projectors learn to use their limited energy wisely and invitations and recognition flow.

The not-self theme of the Projector is bitterness and resentment. The Projector can find themselves in this place when they haven't waited for the invitation or they have accepted the wrong invitation. They may also feel this way when they aren't being seen or when they are doing work—remember the Projector is here to guide.

Projectors are the newest of the types and are here to be the leaders of the next generation. They tap into their wisdom and ability to guide people. Healthy Projectors honor their bodies and realize that rest is part of their process. They understand the potency they have and live by the mantra "Quality over quantity." Finding time alone to dispel the sacral energies of others is necessary for the Projector.

What Does Waiting for the Invitation and Recognition Look Like?

I'm often asked what waiting for the invitation and recognition looks like. Before I dive into that, I want to add that just because you are invited or recognized as a Projector does not mean that the invitation is correct for the Projector. Not every recognition or invitation will be in congruence with their Human Design. The key is to discern which ones are and which ones are not.

I share this because oftentimes Projectors get so bored, desperate, and resentful while waiting that they accept every and any invitation and/or recognition that comes along. Usually, due to their very strong intellect, they have been conditioned by their mind. There is this feeling of "I won't get what I want, so I will settle for this (work, money, relationships)." This is not the correct strategy for a Projector, and settling will often lead them to resistance. In order to discern what is correct for them in life, it would be wise for Projectors to follow their strategy and authority.

Now that the Projector is aware that not every invitation or recognition is for them, let's get into what an invitation or recognition looks like. An invitation may be as straightforward as someone asking a Projector to do something or as veiled as someone saying they love their work. There are lots of shades of gray here when it comes to invitations and recognition with the Projector. Once the invitation or recognition is accepted, the Projector will have the energy to follow through.

As a Projector myself, I like to think about the invitation and recognition as twofold: I want to hear someone ask or recognize me, and I want to feel the authenticity from the other person. Their recognition must be genuine, and I can feel that. If you are curious about what this feels like, think about your favorite client. What is the experience of working with them like? That is what true recognition and invitations feel like. The Projector's energy is fueled by the interaction with the other person.

There is an energy and excitement to this invitation or recognition that over time will dissipate if no decision is reached about moving forward. Therefore, it is important to leverage the Projector strategy and authority when it comes to your decision-making.

This same principle of energy and excitement also applies to relationships over time. A Projector may discern whether that recognition energy is no longer being reciprocated within a relationship, and they may determine this is no longer correct for them.

While Projectors are waiting for this invitation and recognition, it is important to note that it would be in congruence with their design to be pursuing their passions, resting, and being seen. For example, while I am waiting for the invitations and recognition, I am often studying Human Design or heading out into the woods to reset and recharge. I will often share my findings, discoveries, and thoughts on social media or to my email list as a way of allowing myself to be seen.

Many Projectors grapple with being seen; they need to allow themselves to show up in order to get the recognition and invitations they deserve, but they also struggle with having the energy to actually show up. This is tricky because a Projector who is *trying* to be seen can come across as abrasive. Their showing up must come from a place of ease or flow. Otherwise, even if the advice they provide is incredible, people will not be willing to hear it. The act of showing up for a Projector cannot be desperate.

If a Projector is out of congruence with what they are meant to be guiding people on, they will also struggle with being seen as well. This might look like they are showing up, but no one is recognizing them, almost as if they are invisible, or they don't show up at all for fear that no one will recognize them. They can also struggle with being aware of when enough is enough and can get stuck in the on position.

The Not-Self Themes of the Projector

When Human Design Projectors are in their "not-self," they will often experience bitterness and resentment. The not-self happens when a Projector didn't wait for the invitation and is resentful because the person didn't take their advice or when a Projector accepted the wrong invitation. These are just two examples.

When a Projector finds themselves feeling bitter and resentful, it is important to shine awareness on it because it is a clear signal they are out of congruence with their design.

Noticing where and when the bitterness and resentment come up for the Projector is key to getting to the root of the problem. Perhaps, they find it comes up over and over in the same relationship. This could be a work relationship where they know it isn't working out, but they have yet to pull the trigger to put an end to it. This could be a project that they have agreed to do, but it isn't in congruence with their goals, so they feel bitter about having to get it done and do the work.

The reality is when a Human Design Projector is experiencing bitterness or resentment, they are in the not-self. Learning to recognize when they are in the not-self is helpful for the Projector as it allows them to be healthy and live in congruence with their Human Design.

Action Tips & Affirmations for the Projector

If you are a Projector, it is important for you to wait for the invitation and the recognition, otherwise you will be left feeling bitter and resentful that your advice was not heeded.

Your energy is invaluable. Use it intentionally as it is limited.

You are wise beyond your years and are here to guide (manage, direct, advise) others on their journey in whatever form that takes in your life.

You are deeply attuned to the energy of others and enjoy connecting deeply with them.

You can massively impact the lives of others because you know (with great certainty) what others need to be doing in order to make the best use of their energy in their lives and in business. Be sure this advice is met with recognition or invited in, otherwise the recipient may choose to ignore it..

You are not meant to work in the traditional sense of the word. You will find joy in work that balances your need to go deep with others and offers you times of rest and retreat to recharge.

If you attempt to work in the traditional sense of the word, you will often find yourself burned out.

While you wait for your invitations, channel your energy into your passions, and the invitations and recognition will follow.

When you are operating within your strategy, you are magnetic. Invitations and recognition will flow into your life.

It is critical that you carefully select your inner circle. Fill it with people who see you for who you truly are and appreciate your unique ability to see others.

You have a very strong intellect. You study information, people, and events. As a result of this, your mind can be conditioned to believe that you must compromise to get what you want in life. This can result in settling, which can be a huge problem for you. Never settle.

What That Means for Your Business

- Ask open-ended questions to gain clarity.
- Think of social media as a way for you to be invited and recognized. Consistently showing up online will allow you to receive more invitations and gain more recognition. Pick a platform where you can build a community and go deep with your people.
- Choose a business model that allows you to go deep with people over a period of time.
- Build a team that believes in your mission and values your wisdom (and your need to rest).
- Find support with a Generator or Manifesting Generator who is aligned with your core values, believes in your mission, and helps you bridge your energy gaps.
- Reinvent what it means to work. You are here to share your wisdom with the world, but that doesn't mean trading dollars for hours. How can you creatively share your gifts while honoring your energy?

What Does It Mean to Be a Manifestor?

You are a powerful being with a massive capacity to make an impact in the world. Lean into your power with ease. Embrace your free spirit. Own your independence. Fearlessly use your voice. Inform your impact sphere. You are a catalyst for change in this world. Claim it.

THE MANIFESTOR EXPERIENCE

As a Manifestor, you are a catalyst for starting things. This is your superpower. Your energy comes in bursts. You are effective, impactful, and impulsive. You get an idea and want to run with it.

Manifestors are nonenergy beings. They don't have a defined sacral; however, their energy to initiate comes in bursts, and they can power through with their initiations when they are following their strategy and authority. They may, however, skip steps or forget things along the way. Manifestors are the only type that can initiate without waiting (unless you are a Manifestor with emotional authority—more on this later).

Manifestors have a powerful and piercing aura. You can feel the energy of a Manifestor when they walk into a room. They command attention. This can put others on edge because at times the Manifestor can appear to be unpredictable to others. This unpredictability according to others can lend the Manifestor to meet a lot of resistance (and unease), which is why informing becomes especially important.

Manifestors can become conditioned from an early age because they are always trying to initiate, but parents, teachers, and others in authority shut this down. This can lead to a lot of anger for the Manifestor, which ultimately leads them to feeling like a victim because people are always trying to control them when all they want to do is initiate. They feel restricted, powerless, and angry. This is why informing is so important for the Manifestor to help them avoid resistance and take back their power because they are very powerful.

The Manifestor, however, struggles to understand why others would even be concerned with what they are doing since, by nature, Manifestors are very independent. They don't concern themselves with others, which can appear selfish but it's not. Manifestors are unique in their strategy in that they don't need others in order to be in congruence with their strategy whereas the other types need people. For example, a Generator needs others to respond, and a Projector needs invitations and recognition from others.

Manifestors are lone wolves and are happy to go it alone and do it in their way. They are self-contained and have powerful starting energy. When a Manifestor is living their design, they will find themselves in a state of peace. Settled, grounded, and at peace. It is in this place of peace where they will find no resistance or control.

Manifestors may struggle to communicate and may need time alone to get clear. It is in this space of uninterrupted time that they can gain clarity. Manifestors can easily lose their train of thought when speaking with others, so it is important to not interrupt them.

The not-self of the Manifestor is anger. Manifestors may find themselves in the not-self of anger when they have given their power away and are responding instead of initiating. They may also find themselves angry when they have failed to inform key people in their lives and have created resistance for themselves. Anger can also erupt when others try to control the Manifestor. Becoming aware of this anger is helpful in navigating the Manifestor experience and getting back in congruence with the signature goal.

Remember, the Manifestor is here to be a catalyst and make an impact. They yield a great power much different from the other types in the Human Design System. With this power comes great responsibility to use it wisely. Manifestors must learn to leverage their power and bigness in a way that has a positive impact.

Throughout history, there have been many Manifestors who have become dictators. They have wielded their power and charm to get into a position of leadership and then took over control. The Manifestor's power to initiate stands alone in the Human Design. Manifestors were the leaders of the old world. They must learn to use their power to better humanity as a powerful catalyst for change and transformation.

What Does Initiate and Inform Look Like?

The Manifestor strategy is to initiate and inform. Informing does not come naturally to them, and they are the only type where part of their strategy does not come naturally.

Manifestors are here to initiate the other types, especially Generators and Manifesting Generators, into action, while the Projectors are here to guide the process/action along the way. When a Manifestor is initiating, they get an idea and act on it.

Their initiations when in congruence with their strategy and authority (more on Manifestors with emotional and splenic authority later) will give them a burst of starting energy to get into the action. Finding someone to pair with is important to Manifestors so they can finish what they start.

A great example of this is my son, a 1/3 Manifestor, who was looking out his window and saw a tree dancing in the wind. He had the brilliant idea that he wanted to climb that tree. His body took over, his sneakers and coat were on, and outside up the tree he went before anyone knew where he had gone. In this example, it is easy to see that his action without informing may lead to me, as the parent, worrying or even to having a consequence for his action. This lack of informing would create even more resistance for him.

Thankfully, we have opted to parent him to his design, but this is the plight of the Manifestor. If he had informed me of his action, the reaction to his action would have been different. Therefore, many Manifestors are conditioned to either not share their actions because they don't want anyone to change the outcome of what they want to do or to not claim their power of initiating and instead behave as Generators.

This is why informing for the Manifestors is critical for them to live their design. My recommendation is always for Manifestors to have a list of people who are in their inner circle. One for business and one for their personal life. The list is there so that when they have one of their initiations, they don't have to stop and think about who they need to inform. They have a list of who will be impacted by their actions, and they can simply inform those people of their plans. Informing does not mean the Manifestor will change what they are doing, nor should they if it is in congruence with their strategy and authority. It is simply to make others aware and remove turbulence in their key relationships.

Conversely, the Manifestor also likes to be informed by the key people in their lives. Manifestors optimally articulate this to their inner circle so that they can reciprocate the informing to the Manifestor.

When the Manifestor can initiate and inform, it helps them to realize that they do have people who care about them and that they aren't alone. A Manifestor who is out of strategy can feel alone because they, by accident, created a lot of unnecessary turbulence in their relationships.

The Not-Self Themes of the Manifestor

When the Human Design Manifestor is in the not-self, they often experience lots of anger. It is often a result of failing to inform the key parties in their life of their actions, and their actions are met with major resistance and turbulence. They often feel alone, like no one gets them or even likes them.

From my experience, Manifestors are often the most conditioned and in the not-self version of themselves. They often don't associate with being a Manifestor simply because they have shut down their initiating ways for so long. This "makes sense" because parents, schools, and society often try to anchor down the Manifestor and tell them what to do. Manifestors hate this. They like to do things on their terms and very naturally from an early age.

Manifestor children will often see a tree swaying in the yard and run outside to climb it without thinking or worrying about the consequences. This often puts their parents on high alert, and they try to control them even more, which angers the Manifestor. If you are reading this and you are a Manifestor but don't feel like you are one, it is often as a result of conditioning that you have been carrying.

Learning to get back in congruence with your strategy and authority is key. It is best to start by honoring those small urges within that you may feel but ignore from time to time to rebuild a relationship with your strategy. Write down a list of key people to inform once you have an initiation and share with them what you are doing, not for their opinion or input, but simply so they know what you are planning to do.

Action Tips & Affirmations for the Manifestor

You are energetic, powerful, effective, impulsive, and mysterious. You have a unique ability to start and initiate. This could be conversations, business ideas, etc. You can embrace this ability to start without waiting.

You are fiercely independent and are at ease in the solitude of your environment.

You must pair your initiating with informing, especially in relationships. Learning to inform is a key part of your journey. While informing doesn't need to change what you are planning on doing, it will ensure the key parties involved are aware so that they aren't blindsided by whatever new endeavor or idea you have decided to embark on.

You are very internally focused or self-focused and goal-oriented. Understanding and embracing and becoming aware of this will serve you well since most other types are focused on collaboration.

When you embrace your strategy of informing and take note of the key relationships that will be affected by your actions, you show love and respect for the others involved. This goes both ways for Manifestors as they like to be informed by others as well.

Intentionally create breaks and downtime in your work because you are here to initiate, and that initiating energy will run out.

You must discharge the energy of the day that you have collected before your head hits the pillow at night.

You have a deep desire for peace. A place of no resistance or control. You are here to dream and pursue your vision while doing it on your terms.

You are living your strategy when you find yourself in a state of peace. It is when you are living this strategy that you will manifest and make an impact in the world.

You do best when you can let your ideas flow. Inform the key people in your life that interruptions to your train of thought throw you off and that it would be helpful if they could avoid interrupting you when you are in flow.

What That Means for Your Business

- You might find yourself the lone wolf and that's OK. That works for you.

- You will be best suited to a business where you have a clear and definitive start and stop period when working with clients. It is best for you to get in, get the client a transformation, and then get out.

- You have a lot of starting energy; however, that energy can run out when it comes to finishing. Partner up with someone who can help you finish when you inevitably run out of energy.

- You may resist informing others, but often that comes from childhood where you were told no. Realizing that in order to grow your business you need others and then actually informing them of your plan are important aspects of this, otherwise you will burn bridges along the way.

- You can practice your informing through your marketing and social media by sharing what is going on in your business behind the scenes and informing your followers of your next action you plan to take.

- Your energy can be overwhelming to others. It is important to pair up with a Projector who can help guide you on your journey as they can see deeply into others and help you find peace while avoiding anger.

- You often rebel against being controlled, and others worry they will be controlled by you. Informing is your key to avoiding this resistance in business.

What Does It Mean to Be a Generator?

You are here with a purpose. You are fueled and refueled by work that fulfills you. Your inner GPS will guide you on your journey. Trust it. Embrace dancing with life. Become a master of the work you love. Connect with others to fuel your mission. You are a force to be reckoned with. Own it.

THE GENERATOR EXPERIENCE

Generators are in a constant dance with the world. They are here to respond and get to know themselves on a very deep level. Generators, when living in congruence with their strategy and authority, find great joy in doing work they love and are passionate about. They are happy to show up to do this work and feel a deep sense of satisfaction after putting in a day of hard work.

The Generator's energy resets each and every day. This energy, from the sacral, is what moves humanity forward. The Generator is here to go deep and become a master of their work. Much of their happiness is derived and directly connected to doing what they love (and are passionate about).

Generators are here to respond to the world and can become frustrated when they have nothing to respond to. Many Generators have spent most of their lives living as Manifestors and initiating. This inevitably leads to frustration for the Generator. To get back into strategy, the Generator must find something to respond to; this could be a person, a place, a thing, or an event.

All Generators will inevitably hit the "plateau of frustration" when it comes to the work they are doing. This plateau is an opportunity to pause and respond in one of two ways. One, by digging deeper into the work they are already doing, or two, by pivoting. This "plateau of frustration" is a catalyst for the Generator to become even more of an expert and live in pursuit of their purpose. While this plateau carries the not-self theme of the Generator, the energy is slightly different in that the Generator is already doing work they love. Think of this plateau of frustration as a fine-tuning of the work a Generator is here to do. If they are continuing to become more and more of a master, they may in fact hit this plateau more than once.

Generators, once in motion, can work long, focused hours. Transitioning or switching gears is a challenge for the Generator as they are not designed to operate like that. Once a Generator has responded to something, they can then be in the doing for quite some time.

Generators don't do well with open-ended questions, and it is important for Generators to let the key people in their lives know this. Generators do best with yes and no questions that they can use their sacral response to tap into in the now, as the Generator's dance with the universe happens in the now.

Generators have boundless amounts of energy when in their strategy and authority. This life force energy of the Generator needs to burn off. When a Generator is living their signature goal of satisfaction, they go to bed exhausted at the end of the day knowing they did work they loved and were seen for this amazing contribution they have given the world and their relationships.

Generators are deeply relational people, and this is in part due to the defined sacral. Generators thrive in cooperation with others. When Generators are doing work they love, they magnetize people to them. Generators need others in order to be heard since they lack the motor connection to the throat. Generators become empowered when they surround themselves with the right people.

A frustrated Generator is one who is not doing work they love and feels like they are spinning their wheels. The work they are doing becomes more and more frustrating, their energy may no longer reset every day, and they feel a sense of getting nowhere. This is a sign or a goalpost for the Generator to discern. Their sense of satisfaction comes from knowing they made an impact in the world.

What Does Respond and Know Thyself Look Like?

The Generator is unique in that they can trust in their body response of the uh-huh or ut-huh in the now (except for Generators with emotional authority—more on this later). Their sacral is here to provide them with a pulling or a pushing sound response. This response does not come from the throat; it comes from within the diaphragm.

Many adult Generators struggle to connect with their sacral. Have a trusted advisor ask you yes/no questions to help you tap back into this. Don't overthink the answers to the questions. They can start off with simple questions like, "Are you x number of years old?" Or "Your name is ____?" This will help you tap into that feeling of the sacral response.

I love using the example of my four-year-old Generator son, or any Generator children for that matter, since they simply can't help themselves with their full body response. I will never forget the time I asked my four-year-old son whether he wanted to go to the playground. It was a full body "ut-huh." It was loud, confident, and a big headshaking no. He even pulled away from me when I asked him.

This is the sacral response. It's visceral if it is allowed to be. It is the "my head is nodding yes even though my mind hasn't caught up yet" response. It comes from within and has an answer for what is correct in the now. The sacral also might have no response, which means ask me in a different way or ask again later.

Generators have a very good sense of what is right and true for them. They know themselves on a deep level even if they can't discern why or how. Oprah is a Generator. I like to think of it as having a quiet confidence. It just sort of exudes. They have this inner knowing that comes from within that they can trust when it is in response to an outside stimulus.

When Generators are met with crossroads or a decision, it is important for them to pause and then respond. It is in this space of the pause that they can wait for the response. The stimulus for the response may appear in many different ways: a song on the radio, a friend asking a question, a stranger on the street, a sign on the road, or a post on social media. This is the dance with the universe that is part of the Generator experience.

The Not-Self Themes of the Generator

When Human Design Generators are in their not-self, they will often be frustrated. The not-self happens when a Generator doesn't follow their sacral response or they initiate something without first responding.

When a Generator finds themselves feeling frustrated, it is important to shine awareness on it because it is a clear signal they are out of congruence with their Human Design blueprint.

Noticing where and when the frustration comes up for the Generator is key to getting to the root of the problem. Perhaps they find it comes up over and over in the same relationship or work situation.

This could be a project they are working on where step after step they are met with more and more frustration—this is often a sign that they entered into this project without first listening to their sacral response on whether or not this project was correct for them or that they didn't follow their authority. This is especially tricky with emotional authority. Remember, the sacral response is in the here and now—it is a full body yes "uh-huh" or no "ut-huh."

This not-self could be resistance in a relationship because they went ahead and took action on something without first responding or they committed to someone or something they don't love.

The reality is when a Human Design Generator is experiencing frustration, they are in the not-self. Learning to recognize this and come back to home with themselves into their strategy and authority as a Generator is critical to them living in congruence with their Human Design. The Generator will need to get clear on where that frustration erupts so that they can gain clarity and shift out of the not-self by making a different decision next time.

Action Tips & Affirmations for the Generator

You are here to respond to the world not initiate. Your gut response of "uh-huh" or "ut-huh" can help guide you through life. Trust this response.

You are a force to be reckoned with because of the energy you carry with you that resets each and every day. This energy is meant to be used up—daily. Use it.

You have access to a deep inner knowing, and you can trust this inner knowing to guide you. Learn to trust your gut.

You *must* find work that you love and are passionate about. This will be the driving force behind your happiness and joy in life. If you aren't doing work you love, you will become frustrated and your happiness will suffer.

Once you've found work that brings you joy, if you find yourself frustrated, that can often be a place for growth and deeper exploration. For Generators, this can be known as the plateau of growth.

You are here to be an expert, or master. This can be a place for deeper exploration or a time when new opportunities appear. Do not quit when this frustration arrives. Pause and you will find opportunities to respond to.

You do well when you set an intention, visualize the outcome, wait for signs to show up in your reality, and then take action. This pause to respond before taking action is part of the dance Generators must embrace with life. This pause allows you to take a moment and then respond.

You are deliberate and enjoy a methodical process. Switching gears doesn't come easily to you. Honor this.

You are a powerful finisher and can be relied upon to bring projects and activities to life.

What That Means for Your Business

- As a Generator, responding is a way of life for you. Find someone you trust who can ask you yes or no questions so that you can tap into your sacral response and get clear on your path.
- Frustration is often a sign of the need to dig deeper and do more exploration. Rather than giving up, pause. This is a place to dig deeper. You may find yourself frustrated when you are waiting for something to respond to. It can feel unnatural and awkward. Embrace this. You are here to be an expert.
- Social media is your secret weapon as you can find things to respond to. For example, posting an "ask me anything" thread in your community

will give you something to respond to, or asking "What questions do you have about x?" will give you lots of content ideas to then create.

- Most business models will work well for you if you are passionate about the work.
- Surround yourself with people who believe in the work you do, and build a team around your responding.

What Does It Mean to Be a Manifesting Generator?

You are here to create a movement and share your superpowers with the world. You have an innate gift to empower those within your realm. Do the big work that ignites your fire. Oscillate between people and solitude. Embrace your juggling. You are multipassionate, a multitasker, and independent. Trust it.

THE MANIFESTING GENERATOR EXPERIENCE

Manifesting Generators (MGs) can appear to be almost superhuman when compared to the other types in Human Design. They are, as the name suggests, a hybrid of the Manifestor and the Generator. They are multipassionate multitaskers who get more done than the rest of us. They have sustainable energy.

To those who aren't MGs, this multitasking and bouncing from task to task and project to project can almost appear as if they are all over the place. However, this is how an MG is designed to get things done. They can see strategically what needs to get done, and they go and do it. They bounce from thing to thing, moving each forward along the way. They are often told by society that they "should" focus on one thing, but this is incorrect for them. The MG's multitasking ability is their superpower. Pairing multitasking with periods of alone time is a good strategy. MGs need alone time in order to live in congruence with their design.

MGs are designed to do multiple things at once in order to avoid boredom. This is often because their Manifestor (to inform and initiate) self has initiated a bunch of projects and their Generator self is working hard to work through them even though they have not responded, which is the Generator's theme (to respond). MGs, when they don't follow their strategy, can find themselves working simply to work.

An MG's weakness is that they often find themselves skipping steps, which means they must go back and redo things. At times, this can be frustrating, costly, and painful for the MG. Becoming aware that this is the MG's tendency and finding someone to support in the missed steps can be helpful. This might also mean they start things and don't always finish them.

MGs have the incredible gift of being able to impact those around them. Since they have a defined sacral, there is a relational vibrance that radiates from them. Martin Luther King Jr. was an MG. His people stood beside him. He didn't stand alone. This is the way of the MG.

MGs also give those around them the gift of empowerment. Because of their connection from their sacral to their throat, their very presence empowers those around them. The MG simply existing gives others this sense of empowerment.

MGs can also act on their own. They don't necessarily need others, and it is often faster for them to do it on their own. MGs are both relational and willing to go it alone. They are both empowering in their energy and inspiring to others in all that they achieve. Learning to balance their independence with their need for others is a big challenge for MGs.

With the seemingly endless amount of energy the MG has, there is no limit to the amount they can create. If they have responded and received a yes, they can stay in creation mode almost endlessly.

An MG's signature goals are satisfaction and peace. They feel a deep sense of being grounded when they are impacting people, doing work they love, and giving life to their multiple passions. Like the other types, there is a duality to the MG and their not-self theme is anger and frustration. A very powerful combo. This can happen to the MG when they are not doing work they love, doing work that makes them feel like they are spinning their wheels, or taking part in relationships that are too controlling or when they are stuck waiting for something to respond to. MGs have the opportunity to use this frustration and anger as a place to learn and understand where they need to get back into congruence with their purpose and design.

The MG energy, like the Generator energy, is meant to be used up each and every day—think of it like trying to bottle up a lightning bolt. The energy is incredibly powerful and hard to keep contained. When MGs don't use up their energy every day, their health can suffer, particularly their thyroid.

What Does Visualizing, Responding, and Informing Look Like?

For the MG, their strategy is to visualize, pause, respond, and then inform. First, they visualize their idea and the outcome that they are hoping to achieve. Once they have visualized the idea, next comes the pause or the waiting before taking action. This is where they are waiting for something to respond to, which could be a person, a sign, or something external. This is like the Generator in that it will be an "uh-huh" or "ut-huh" from within. Their response will come from within, almost as a push (no) or a pull (yes) depending upon the response. I'm told that when it is a yes, the feeling is almost as if the body lights up. Lastly, the MG, like the Manifestor, needs to inform the key parties.

Like with all the types, if you have emotional authority, there is a caveat here (which we will get into later). Just know that with emotional authority, you need to ride your emotional wave before making your final decision, then inform. While this adds a layer of complexity to the MG's process, it will help eliminate resistance, frustration, anger, and regret in their lives.

Many MGs end up being busy doing nothing because they have been made to believe they are Manifestors for most of their life, and they go about life initiating instead of responding. MGs don't like to pause or slow down, so waiting for something to respond to can be torture for many of them.

It is in this pause that the MG can get clarity around what is right for them by tapping into their sacral response (see Generators for more on this). Yes/no questions are helpful for MGs who are looking to gain clarity. Relying on a trusted friend or adviser to ask the MG these questions can prove to be helpful as this gives them something to respond to.

Once the MG has a clear response, this is where informing begins. Like the Manifestor, they need to inform the key parties in their lives of the action they plan to take. This means creating a list of the people who will be impacted by their actions and then letting them know of their plans. The informing does not mean that their actions will change; it is simply notifying other people of what they plan to do.

The Not-Self Themes of the Manifesting Generator

When Human Design MGs are in their not-self, they will often experience anger and frustration. The not-self happens when an MG didn't follow their sacral response or they initiated without informing.

When an MG finds themselves feeling anger and frustration, it is important to shine awareness on it because it is a clear signal they are out of congruence with their Human Design blueprint.

Noticing where and when the anger and frustration come up for the MG is key to getting to the root of the problem. Perhaps, they find it comes up over and over in the same relationship or work situation.

This could be a project they are working on and step after step they are met with more and more frustration—this is often a sign that they entered into this project without first listening to their sacral response on whether or not this project was correct for them.

This could be anger and resistance in a relationship because they went ahead and took action on something without first informing the key parties involved in the project.

The reality is when a Human Design MG is experiencing frustration and/or anger, they are in the not-self. Learning to recognize this and come back to home to their strategy and authority as an MG **is critical to them living in congruence with their Human Design.**

Action Tips & Affirmations for the Manifesting Generator

You are uniquely capable of getting more done than most. You have an incredible ability to move fast and adapt. You are able to sustain your energy for long periods of time.

You thrive when you multitask, and this multitasking is an essential part of your process.

You find yourself happiest when you have time to visualize your ideas. This allows you to try them on first before taking action. Once you have visualized, pause, inform, then take action.

You are here to create, do, and make an impact.

You like momentum and going fast, so informing can oftentimes feel like you are stepping out of that momentum; however, when you inform, you decrease the resistance you might feel from others and you decease the risk of damaging a key relationship.

You are part Manifestor and part Generator, so finding the balance between visualizing an initiation, idea, or action, pausing, and then responding will be an important step in your journey. This will feel unnatural to you, but embrace the discomfort of it. It will ultimately lead you to finding more joy and responding to the right things along the way.

You are very well equipped to work in fast-paced environments that require you to switch gears from thing to thing or person to person. Find a business that allows you to do this.

Own your process and don't feel the need to explain it to others. They won't understand your way of juggling lots of things, and that is OK.

You are highly capable of moving very fast, while most other people around you will not be able to move so quickly. Learning to be patient with the speed of others will be important along your journey, especially in business.

What That Means for Your Business

- You are meant to be multitasking; this is a key part of your process. Embrace it and don't feel like you have to explain yourself (or your process) to others.

- As you are growing your business, there is a pull to do lots of different things and try on lots of different business models—stay focused on one model. Channel your multitasking energy into creating strategic relationships and offering your services in different ways within the context of these relationships. For example, find a collaboration where you can teach a different group of people.

- Workshops and masterclasses are a great way for you to channel your multitasking energy if you are feeling bored with your one business model.

- You may, in fact, want to offer your clients multiple ways in which you show up for them. Some days you may feel like teaching, other days you may feel like voxing, and some days you may be inspired to write.

- Find ways in which you can pair tasks together; for example, answering your Voxer messages while going for a walk or doing a weekly walk and talk with a client. Dual-purposed activities serve you well.

- Social media is a great tool that you can use to test out your new ideas. Have something you've been visualizing? Inform people on social media about it and see what you receive as feedback.

- Find someone to support you with the details. You move fast and can miss details along the way. Find a Generator who will pick up the pieces along the way for you.

- Running your first course live so that you can get feedback is a good idea, as you thrive off of the feedback.

- Putting up a waitlist, gauging interest, and then creating the "thing" is a great strategy for you!

What Does It Mean to Be a Reflector?

You are a powerful being with a massive capacity to make an impact in the world. Lean into your power with ease. Embrace your free spirit. Own your independence. Fearlessly use your voice. Inform your impact sphere. You are a catalyst for change in this world. Claim it.

THE REFLECTOR EXPERIENCE

Reflectors have no defined centers within their Human Design chart. They are truly unique beings in that they are incredibly impacted by their environment. They are mirrors for the rest of us about our authenticity (mind, body, spirit) as they mirror the community they surround themselves with. Their uniqueness comes from the gates that are activated within their Human Design chart, and this brings personality to their being.

Reflectors account for less than 1 percent of the population and can be deeply conditioned by others because of all of the openness in their chart. They are fluid human beings who can change from moment to moment, almost like a chameleon adapting and changing to the environment around them.

Reflectors are a gift for the other types as they are a mirror showing us where we are flawed or inauthentic. Reflectors see each of us for who we truly are, which can cause them to feel a great sense of disappointment for humanity.

Since Reflectors act as a mirror, they can tune up and magnify the energy of others and support others in living in more congruence with who they are truly meant to be. Reflectors have a unique gift to sense when others are truly meant and ready to be seen and can use their gifts to support them in becoming more of who they are by reflecting back to them.

I like to think of Reflectors as old souls. They are wise guides, here to show us who we are. They mirror back to us our strengths, weaknesses, and flaws. They see the highs and lows of the human experience. They feel the depths of the human experience. Their auras sample the energy of others, discerning whether they are ready to step into their own uniqueness.

The Reflector's environment is incredibly important for them to be healthy and live in congruence with their strategy and authority. Finding the "right" environment for them is a key part of their journey. This could mean a physical location like their home, the nature that surrounds them, or a specific location in the world. This also includes building and/or being part of a community that feels good to them.

Time in nature is very helpful for the Reflector to dispel the energy of others. The Reflector can discern where this place is for themselves and make spending time there a part of their regular practice. This will help them maintain their sense of self and stay congruent with their design.

When a Reflector is in their signature goal, they feel a sense of excitement and wonder about humanity. They are surprised by the other types as Reflectors are living out their authentic selves and perhaps even invited in to participate if it feels correct for them. Their not-self theme of disappointment is diminished, and they are living in the moment filled with awe about the potential of humanity.

Famous Reflectors include Sandra Bullock, Scott Hamilton, James Frey, and Richard Burton.

What Does Waiting a Lunar Cycle Look Like?

As the only lunar type, a Reflector's strategy is to wait a lunar cycle—twenty-eight days—before making decisions. Reflectors must be invited into the decision-making process by others. They cannot invite themselves. Once they are invited in to make a decision, they must wait a full twenty-eight days in order to gain clarity.

The reason behind this is they have no fixed decision-making process within their chart, and they need the consistency of the twenty-eight days as the moon cycles around the sixty-four gates within the Human Design chart for them to come to a decision. Waiting for the cycle of the sixty-four gates helps them gain clarity.

A Reflector has no inner authority, so it is in this waiting twenty-eight days and talking about their intentions with others that they gain clarity. Reflectors gain clarity by talking out their decisions and having those decisions reflected back to them in others.

Reflectors are encouraged to have a consistent group of friends who can mirror back to them. This consistency will help the Reflector feel good, know they have a listening ear, and support the Reflector in their decision-making process.

Part of the Reflector process is to discern when they are feeling good. It is in this feeling good that they can be assured that a decision is correct for them. When Reflectors are in the right place with the right people, they will know that this is right for them. If they are not feeling good, then that is a clear sign that they need to make a change.

Once the Reflector has waited twenty-eight days to make a big decision, they can then do whatever they want. There is no more waiting required after the twenty-eight days.

Reflectors thrive in healthy communities and being around people who help them feel really good. Reflectors, especially more than the other types, need people. They also need time alone to discharge the energy of others.

The Not-Self Themes of the Reflector

When Reflectors are in the not-self, they will experience disappointment. This sense of disappointment comes from their interaction with other people. Since Reflectors take in the energy of those around them and amplify it, they feel both the highs and lows of the human experience. Reflectors may be in this not-self because they were not included.

Reflectors thrive on being part of healthy communities. A healthy community allows the Reflector to experience excitement and delight (the highs of the human experience). Conversely, when a Reflector is in the not-self, that theme of disappointment will be present. This includes disappointment in the people around them (the lows of the human experience), along with disappointment about not being included or asked to partake in the community.

For many Reflectors, spending time outdoors is necessary. This time in nature allows them to dispel the energy of others and tap back into themselves.

Action Tips & Affirmations for the Reflector

You are a truly unique and special human being who is wise beyond your years. You often march to the beat of your own drum.

You are designed to live in the moment and find joy in the newness that each day brings. Live in the wonder of this very moment. The wonder of "who am I today?" and "will I be surprised, included, or invisible today?" which is life as a Reflector.

You are a beacon of joy and happiness, and you spread light wherever you go.

You are best served when you can find or create a community that supports you.

You are here to be a mirror to others and reflect back and/or amplify the energy of others.

You have a keen awareness of when others are not living within their strategy or not living up to their potential as humans.

Finding the right place, the right people, at the right time is key to unlocking happiness for you.

You are here to support others in finding their potential. While that might appear in different ways for others, it is important to embrace this gift.

Getting to know who you are and becoming wise about your inner workings and the process that intertwines you with others is important to your success. It will allow you to remain wide open to what is passing through you. There will be blips or something unusual going on around you, which is an aspect of your gift. Learning to identify this is helpful to finding your joy.

You are here to sample life and experience all of it in its totality.

Place plays a critical role in your journey. Place can mean both your home or a place to burn off your energy, as well as your place of business. Finding a community to call home is one of the most important decisions you face, and it must be met with discernment while honoring your process of waiting twenty-eight days before making a decision.

What That Means for Your Business

- Find a business BFF who will sit and listen to you so that you can find clarity. Talking things out is a great way for you to find clarity.
- Being consistent can be a challenge for you, so having a support team and system will help you thrive.
- Think of your social media as a way to create your own community where you can thrive. This can allow you to bring your incredible vision to life, surrounded by people who live and breathe the same values as you. Use your social media to share the depth of your being—your joy and your sorrow—in a way that feels good to you.
- Audio is a great way for you to express yourself in the world since it brings you clarity. Keep this in mind with your marketing efforts.
- Building a business that has built-in downtime on a regular basis is essential for your success as you need to mindfully discharge the energies of others.

PROFILES IN THE WILD

In this chapter, we are diving into the profile (lines—i.e., 1/3, 4/6/ 2/4, 5/1, etc.) within your Human Design blueprint. The profile gives vibrance to the personality you present to the world and what those interactions will look like. It creates guardrails with how you learn best, the experiences of learning, and how your personality interacts with the world around you.

You could think of this as almost the different characters within a story or the Jungian archetypes. You might have a hero, a joker, an everyman, etc., or if we were to continue the lighthouse metaphor, your type is the frame or foundation of the lighthouse, and your profile is the colors the lighthouse is painted and what the exterior of the lighthouse looks like to others.

There are twelve different profiles in Human Design, which consist of six different combinations of the six lines. The combination of the lines that make up our profile color who we are. With each profile, there are two different numbers; for example, 3/5. The first number, 3, is in our conscious personality, while the second number, 5, is derived subconsciously.

As we dive into the content, you may find that you do not relate to your second line. I find that when you shine awareness on what it is, you can more clearly see how it has influenced your life. I believe that as we age, we truly become more of ourselves. The second line in our profile becomes more apparent. So, if you don't relate to your second line, know that that is normal. As we dive into the content, you may find you become more aware of how the second line has colored your life thus far. It is in this shining a light on it that you will create more vibrance which you can more clearly see and become aware of.

Profiles in Human Design are leveraged so that we can better understand how we are designed to interact with the world. Our profiles are made up of two separate parts:

1. the design side (red in a traditional Human Design chart or on the right side), also known as the subconscious side or the body side
2. the personality side (black in a traditional Human Design chart or on the left side), also known as the conscious side or the mind side

When thinking about the lines in Human Design, it is important to think about using the metaphor of a house. The first line is the foundation upon which the house is built. The second line is the first floor of the house. The third line is the stairs or the transition from the first floor to the second floor. The forth line is the second story or the second story foundation. The fifth line is the mysterious second story curtained window or some refer to it as the attic, and the sixth line is the roof of the house. The first three lines or the lower trigram are often concerned with themselves and their process is very personal. They tend to not rush when externalizing things and often don't want much to do with others. The upper lines or upper trigram are transpersonal or interpersonal (I talk more about this nuance in the workbook) and have an outer directed process. These roles essentially need to share with others. Share the past, share the future, create change.

It is important to note that with respect to the lines, there are intrapersonal and transpersonal themes. With the first three lines—1, 2, and 3—the theme is intrapersonal. The energy of these lines is more self-focused. With any of these lines in the profile, you are more concerned about your own personal experiences and have an understanding of life through yourself.

The second three lines—4, 5, and 6—are transpersonal lines. This means that these people are more focused on having experiences through relationships, and therefore, they need others. By design, there will be certain people who are more concerned with themselves, and their own experiences and others who will be concerned about relationships. There will also be some profiles in tension with one other, having one intrapersonal line and one transpersonal.

The six lines in the Human Design System are listed below. The first name you will see is the formal name given by the founder of Human Design, while the second name is what I like to use.

- Line 1—Investigator or Researcher
- Line 2—Hermit or Introvert
- Line 3—Martyr or Experimenter
- Line 4—Opportunist or Mayor
- Line 5—Heretic or Disruptor
- Line 6—Role Model or Mentor

The twelve profiles that make up the Human Design System are as follows:

- 1/3 Investigator Martyr
- 1/4 Investigator Opportunist
- 2/4 Hermit Opportunist
- 2/5 Hermit Heretic
- 3/5 Martyr Heretic
- 3/6 Martyr Role Model
- 4/6 Opportunist Role Model
- 4/1 Opportunist Investigator
- 5/1 Heretic Investigator
- 5/2 Heretic Hermit
- 6/2 Role Model Hermit
- 6/3 Role Model Martyr

Now that you know the six different lines that make up the twelve different profiles, it is important to note that certain lines have more synergy than others. The following lines are synergistic:

- Lines 1 and 4
- Lines 2 and 5
- Lines 3 and 6

This simply means that the themes of these lines have more in common, and there is more ease and tranquility within the profiles.

Other lines will experience more dissonance, resistance, or tension. As an example, the 2, which is the hermit who is happy to stay in their own bubble, will always be in tension with the 4, as it seeks a network or inner circle of people. The following lines will have tension or dichotomy:

- Line 1 will have tension with Line 5 and Line 6.
- Line 2 will have tension with Line 4 and Line 6.
- Line 3 will have tension with Line 4 and Line 5.

Now you might be thinking to yourself, *Well, there is a dichotomy within my profile, does that mean I am destined for a life with drama?* Absolutely not. This is just something to bring awareness to as you might feel a divide within yourself at times. For example, with the 6/2 profile, the 6 is here to help each of us be our best selves, while the 2 thrives on alone time. These two things are at odds with one another. This simply means the individual will need others and will want to be with them, but they will also crave alone time. It is about learning to honor the pull within the profiles.

Before we begin . . .

A Note about the Personality/Mind/Conscious Line and the Design/Body/Subconscious Line

One thing I like to keep in mind when thinking about profiles it that while we are whole beings, I find it important to recognize that the two lines in our profile make up how different parts of our being are designed to operate. For example, if we are looking at a 3/5 profile. The 3 is in the personality, mind, conscious side—first number in the profile and the right-hand (often colored black) side of the chart. This means that is how my mind is designed to behave—the personality I bring into my interactions with others. Remember, the mind is here in service of others. This means that the 3 is designed to operate in service of others in Human Design. While my 5 line is here to determine how my body or subconscious is designed to operate—the second number, left-hand (often red) side of the chart. This means my body operates as a fifth line.

Please remember one cannot operate without the other. They are both parts of a greater whole, and the whole is woven together. It is integrated; one side cannot exist without the other. The 3/5 or any lines of a profile exist together. While you may feel inclined to pull them apart, I encourage you not to. Yes, I bring this up so you can look at them separately, but in looking at your own chart, you must synthesize the information together. How does the 3 of my mind operate with the 5 of my body? How do these two separate parts when woven together operate to form something new?

In my experience, many people, especially adults, are more reliant on their mind or conscious line than their body line. Whereas children often lean far more into their body and very naturally use their mind in service of others as we are designed to unless, of course, they take on conditioning.

Conditioning isn't inherently good or bad. It can be good. It can be bad. It can be nothing, and it is happening all the time. It can come from the people we surround ourselves with, from simply existing on this earth, from society, from the movies we watch, from the books we read, from the things we listen to, etc. More important to note with conditioning though is to simply be aware that it is happening. In our western culture, we are taught from a very early age to rely on our minds instead of our bodies, even though our bodies carry forth a well of wisdom for us to learn from. We override our intuitive nudges with sensemaking. We feel a knowing in our gut, yet we default to our mind. And our mind serves a purpose. It is here to keep us safe, to meet our foundational safety needs. It keeps us safe from the threat of a bear attack or from trusting (or not) a stranger. The reality in our world today is the mind doesn't serve the same purpose as it did back in the early ages. The mind is here to be in service of the other, yet more often than not, we lean on it for ourselves, and it often causes us to get way out of whack.

LINE 1—INVESTIGATOR A.K.A. RESEARCHER

There is always something more to learn—a depth of knowledge hiding in the abyss for those who are willing to discover it.

Affirmation: I honor my need to have a solid foundation and prioritize this so that I can pursue my need to research and explore. I am here to follow my curiosity wherever it may take me. I dig deep. I am a master of my craft and honor the time it takes to establish expertise so that I feel confident. Allow me the space to follow my explorations without interruptions. I am deeply methodical in my process and am slow to embrace change due to the fact I love to research. I have a thirst for knowledge and understanding. Change for me comes slowly as I figure things out. I study, observe, discern, plan, and then decide. I trust that I have acquired enough knowledge to ebb and flow with the changes of life. I am a wealth of information and a resource for others. People respect my knowledge and seek out my opinion since I am so knowledgeable.

The Researcher

P rofiles include 1/3, 1/4, 4/1, 5/1.

The Line 1 or first line is here to figure things out, investigate, research, and explore. If you have a one in your profile, you are here to get to the bottom of things. You will thrive in the process of figuring things out, and it is in this process of figuring things out that you build the confidence to stand in your purpose.

In order for you to fully embody your researcher tendencies, it is important for you to first establish a solid foundation in life. If you think of Maslow's hierarchy of needs, this would be the foundation of physiological and safety needs, which include food, water, shelter, career, property, and health. Once these have been established, the researcher can then relax and move on to living their purpose and spending the time they desire digging deep and becoming an expert.

As a first line, you might be slow to adapt to change or to try new things. This is because of your inner yearning to have all the information before changing. This may be something as simple as buying a new mattress, which you need to research extensively, or it may be launching a new program where you must have all the information in the content of the program and the ways to launch figured out before you can begin. You may never feel fully ready to make that decision because there is so much to research. Learning to balance the yearning for information with the need to move forward is critical to living a fulfilled life, especially with the littler things in life.

You are truly an expert or a master. You have a depth of knowledge. This is because you give yourself the permission to study and research until you know enough especially when it comes to your purpose and career. This depth of knowledge distinctly positions you in a different way from the other lines. You are often niche in your information, and while you may see this as a detriment to your progress, it is a gift to the world.

Your process is full of introspection, and you show others what you believe they need to see. You have a sharp awareness of others, in part because you study others first and then act accordingly. You rarely play your hand first, but you wait for others to do so. This can make you—the first line—appear chameleon-like.

In your pursuit of understanding, you develop empathy for others, but you don't like to rock the boat. You are often overprepared, and you have a need to know what to expect. You like clear expectations and can loathe surprises as they make you feel uneasy.

Change does not come easy to the first line researcher. It makes you feel like you don't know enough. It creates unease and unrest for you. Communicating this to those in your life is helpful in alleviating some of this tension. While we can never eliminate the unknowns or the changes we experience in life, shining awareness of how these changes make them feel can be supportive to the first line.

You will have a need to be alone while you research. You do not like to be interrupted in your process, and it bothers you when others interrupt this precious discovery time for you. Being clear about what you are doing can allow others to be supportive so this sacred time is uninterrupted.

Your depth of knowledge is a gift to the world, and the other types will seek you out. You are a beacon of understanding; your knowledge runs deep and will only run deeper as you age. Your confidence over time grows because you have a better understanding of how the world works.

Line 1—Distilled

- Identifies with the following traits: Introspection, Chameleon, Empathy
- Like to discover how life works
- Like to get to the bottom of things—"figure it out"
- Must have a secure foundation for success (key to being able to relax)
- Tend to be deeply empathetic
- Tend to be introspective in their learning—"Don't bother me; I'm exploring"
- Seek out masters or experts and/or they become one
- Study other people's behavior
- Show others what they believe they want to see
- Is keenly aware and can act accordingly
- Struggle with change and change can be very uncomfortable for them
- Run a hyperniched business, if in business

LINE 2—HERMIT
A.K.A. INTROVERT

There are seasons in life. There is solace in solitude. There is brilliance in blossoming. There is a yearning for this duality.

Affirmation: I thrive in my own little world. This world is perfectly curated for and suited to me. It gives me life and fuels my energy. The more I hide, the more others crave my energy and recognize me for my gifts. It is through their recognition that I can clearly see myself and the impact I make on the world. My energy is most vibrant when I honor my pull to be alone and regularly indulge in the practice of alone time. I do things in my own way with my own process, and I have let go of explaining this way to others as it is not for them (and I likely cannot explain it). I am a master of balance in relationships and a master of avoiding drama. My brilliance, talent, and genius are abundant, though I might not always see it. I allow others to see these gifts in me. It is through this seeing I embody my gifts and live my purpose.

The Introvert

Profiles include 2/4, 2/5, 5/2, 6/2.

You are much like the seed waiting for spring to arrive. Once planted in the ground, you wait and wait while the sun shines down on you warming the soil, and others tend to you, waiting for you to sprout. At just the right moment, you sprout. Over time, you blossom into the beautiful flower or fruit you were meant to be, but only because someone else recognized that you were just waiting to be planted. You blossom only after periods of solitude.

As the second line introvert, you need others in order to recognize your talents and the genius that you bring to the table. You are naturally talented, and your talent comes easy to you. You don't necessarily see it or recognize it as talent, which is why you need others to recognize it for you.

You hide out and thrive in your own space. Your environment is important to you. Cultivating a home or space that feels good to you is critical. This space is where you refuel, where you find solace, and where you truly thrive. This space is energy giving and is your own. You mindfully select the many details of the space.

Spending time alone is easy for you. In fact, you often prefer to be alone. The vibrancy you emanate is rooted in the quality of your alone time. This keeps your energy thriving.

The duality of the second line is that the more time you spend alone and hiding out, the more others will be drawn to you. All second lines are paired with a transpersonal line, so there is this constant tension in your being since you need others in order to fulfill your purpose, but you crave being alone. It is in this dichotomy you exist.

As you are called upon by others and recognized for your genius (natural talents), you will be pulled from your environment to be seen. Much like the flower or fruit tree mentioned above. You will showcase your talents and then retreat and come back again. It is in this cycle that the second line truly thrives. You burst out into the world for the right experiences and then hibernate to regenerate and renew—honoring your need for alone time, sharing your genius with the world, and then hiding again. The metaphor of the flower or fruit tree is a great example here in that the introvert follows seasons in their life.

Most second lines will struggle to explain the reasoning behind how or why you do the things that you do. Others will often be curious about this, but you often very genuinely cannot explain it. So having others respect the introvert's process is important. You can't explain, and even if you could, you don't want to.

You are autonomous and don't like to rock the boat with others. You have a keen sense of balance and hate being put in the middle. You have a keen ability to tell others what they like to hear in order to keep balance. You do this in part because you simply crave your solitude and prefer to avoid drama. You care, but you are mindful of where you invest your energy.

The people who are in your close relationships respect your need for alone time and solitude. You will often want to be around people who are also comfortable being alone. Your alone time is sacred, and you don't like to be yanked out of it. Communicating this to those around you is supportive to you especially in business since your creativity and natural gifts in the world are regenerated during this time.

You have natural gifts to share with the world, and you simply need to bloom when the timing is right. You have a keen awareness that you need others in order to see the genius and talents you bring to the world. You honor your instinct to be alone. You cultivate an environment where you effortlessly regenerate when you embrace solitude and wait for spring to come again.

Line 2—Distilled

- Identifies with the following words: The Natural, Projection, Democrat
- Are like a seed waiting to awaken, grow, and produce its own unique fruit
- Are noted for their natural talents and genius
- Love their alone time
- Rely on others to call them out to better understand their gifts and genius
- Are self-contained—like to be left alone to do their thing
- Do not like to have to explain how or why they do what they do (often they cannot explain either)
- Can play both sides well because they don't want to invest their energy in taking sides
- Love their own environment
- Rely on the right energetic call to live out their purpose

LINE 3—MARTYR
A.K.A. EXPERIMENTER

*There are no mistakes, only wisdom to embody
from lessons learned.*

*Affirmation: My life is a series of experiments that give
me lessons to share with the world. I share my experiments with others in order to show a better way with
more ease. I embrace taking the long road and find joy
in the peaks and valleys of my experiences. I am NOT
the sum of my experiments (good or bad, up or down,
high or low), but rather I experience the world through
these experiments. They give me resilience, wisdom
beyond my years, and depth. Many will call my experiments mistakes; they are not mistakes but are how I
make sense of the world and find understanding. I make
no mistakes. I only find a better way for others (usually
quite quickly) by pointing out what is not working. I use
this superpower to create change in the world. I boldly
stand up for what I believe. I let go of feeling like I am the
sum of my mistakes and embody the wisdom from the
lessons I have endured. I am an experiential learner, and*

my experiences provide understanding, which fuels the wisdom that I share with the world. I am sought out for the wisdom I have embodied.

The Experimenter

Profiles include 1/3, 3/5, 3/6, 6/3.

The Line 3 (third line—experimenter) bumps into life, and life bumps into it. As a third line, you take what appears to others to be the long road or the trying road. You may fumble, flail, falter, and fail, but this is your process. Your trials and tribulations serve as the way in which you experience the world in order to give wisdom to the other profiles.

I say this from experience as a fellow third line experimenter: you are not your failures, your trials and tribulations, or the challenges you face along the way. It is simply how you are here to learn. It is through this experiential learning that you gain wisdom beyond your years to share with others. This wisdom you gain will be sought out by others in order to help them do more in less time. You share with them your experiences and experiments. It is in this discovery process that you learn what is practical, truly useful, and effective.

You are here to point out and discover what does not work. Your trial and error gives you this wisdom. Prior to age forty, you will often jump into every new experience that comes your way; however, by the time you hit forty, you will have a greater awareness of what feels good to experiment with and what does not feel good. This will mean that your incessant need to experiment will subside, and you will have a deeper awareness of what you'd like to experiment with. Your experiments from your youth with give depth to your wisdom from here on out in life. Your yearning to experience something new will still be present, but you will simply be more discerning because of the wisdom you've gained thus far.

You will often point out and recognize what does not work faster than other people do. This energy can bring challenges to your relationships as you are quick to pull the plug on things you see aren't working—which can include relationships. The best relationships for you, especially those in your inner circle, are ones that give you the freedom and space to go through your experiments. In relationships, over time you gain clarity by going slow—this avoids disappointment on your end, and this will allow you to discern which relationships are correct for you. This softens the bonds made and broken theme that can often plague your relationships.

Your experimentation process creates a resilience in you. You are quick on your feet, quick to adapt, and thrive in challenging the status quo. You see things faster than others, and as a result, you are a massive catalyst for change in the world. Your wisdom makes you a leader, and if others want to know how to do something, you are the best person to ask. You have tried everything. You learn through the experiences you've had that didn't work, and this gives depth to your wisdom. You make *no* mistakes in your life as each experiment is a place where you learn and gain wisdom and knowledge.

Your resilience will lead you to stand up for what you believe in and position you as a leader. You challenge the old and welcome the new. You are a force that drives change for the greater good in the world. You may be told you have wisdom beyond your years or are an old soul. Honoring your need for space and freedom is critical. Appreciating your discernment for what does not work while learning to realize its impact will always be a balancing act. Learn to soften the blow of your discernment of what's not working by communicating clearly.

You are truly a force when you are living in congruence with your design. You are wise about the world and will be sought after for your guidance, wisdom, and experiences.

Line 3—Distilled
- Trial and Error, Mutation, Adaption
- Are able to easily discover what does not work
- Find ways to enjoy the experimental process of trial and error
- Are catalysts for change in the world
- Have a natural resilience and adaptability
- Enjoy challenging the status quo and figuring out what does not work
- Are quick to say, "This is not true" and stand up for it
- Notice what is not working faster than anyone else—can lead to a bonds made and broken theme

- Have an inherent need for space and freedom in all that they do, especially in relationships
- Don't like to be controlled
- Are natural and resilient leaders, especially after the age of forty
- Experiment less and settle down after forty and become more clear about what does and does not need to be experimented with

LINE 4—OPPORTUNIST
A.K.A. MAYOR

There is a drive for connection that lives within—it colors the vibrance of our lives and the power of our communities.

Affirmation: I am driven by the people in my life. They are the foundation and source of growth in my life. Change for me must be slow, deliberate. I wait and wait for the right opportunities, and once I am well prepared, with great certainty I leap. Accept me for who I am without trying to change me. My care for others runs deep as I tie my worth to my network and the people in it. I am friendly to many and close with few. My inner circle is the catalyst for the growth in my world as they connect me to new people. It is through these introductions that I thrive in all areas of life and I am better able to live my purpose. I am consistent, stable, and reliable.

The Mayor

Profiles include 1/4, 2/4, 4/1, 4/6.

As a fourth line, you are friendly with everyone, but your close relationships or inner circle are incredibly important to you. Your network is your biggest asset, and you will find most of your success in life is derived from your social network. You do not do well with new people. People who are new to your world or ecosystem need to come to you through referral or introduction.

Your relationships run deep, and you care very deeply as well. You are influential, and people believe in your mission. You have a gift for influencing others who come into your network through your inner circle.

You may have an inner circle for business and another for personal. These steady relationships are your lifeblood. As the mayor, you tend to be friendly to everyone and close with few. You are a master networker, and connecting with others comes easily, especially on a human level.

Change, however, doesn't come easily to you. You resist it and are very rarely ready for change. Creating foundations in all areas of your life is important to you. This will often mean you won't leave one job until you have another lined up. Same goes for relationships. You like to have another foundation in place before you give up the one you currently have. The unknown makes you uneasy and uncomfortable.

You yearn to be accepted as you are in all your relationships. Since you don't like change, you don't want others to change you. You accept others as they are for all their flaws, quirks, and individuality. You expect the same in return.

At your healthiest, you are consistent, reliable, and stable, and you are a good friend who can be relied upon. People who were your friends years ago can pick up the phone to chat with you and it will seem like you haven't missed a beat.

The fourth line may struggle to communicate or be afraid to say their truth. This can look like a fourth line simply creating another alternative and then moving on without dealing with the challenges or communicating their discontent.

The fourth line blossoms when they are leveraging their network to grow. For example, if a fourth line were to walk up to someone and pitch them, they would likely be rejected; however, a fourth line thrives when people who need what they have to offer come to them through an introduction or a referral. This is the way for the fourth line to thrive—referrals and introductions. This is not just in business either. This is in all areas of life.

The quality of a fourth line's life and impact is in direct correlation to their network. So cultivating the correct network becomes a large part of the journey for those with a 4 in their profiles.

Embracing this strategy of relying on others is an important part of living your design and being in congruence with your purpose. When you realize this is the best way for you as a fourth line, you decrease a lot of resistance along the way. Your relationships will flow, and referrals will become abundant when you embody this part of your design.

Your investment of energy in relationships is meant to be reciprocal, and it's important that you receive a return on investment (which might not be monetary). It is key for you to ensure you get out what you put into your relationships. For example, if someone is always taking or asking too much from a relationship, then you will likely feel frustrated. Alternatively, if you are taking too much from a relationship, it will likely weaken. Again, your life is in direct correlation to your relationships, so do what you need to do in order for them to thrive.

Time alone or retreating is important for the fourth line as is their environment. Be mindful of how much time you are spending with your network. You will likely need time to retreat after periods of connection. Having a stable environment that feels good during this retreat will allow you to refuel potentially faster.

You are a powerful influence in your community.

Line 4—Distilled
- Externalization, Friendliness
- Concerned with the foundation of human relationships
- Are deeply influential
- Have a gift for networking and is incredibly friendly
- Have a quality of life that is in direct proportion to their network
- Have a sphere of influence that is limited to already established relationships—Think referrals or introductions
- Require times of retreat to nurture themselves
- Must get a return on investment from their energy investment

- Must transition from one relationship to another before letting it go
- Can feel great angst when faced with the unknown
- Move slowly and methodically—don't change quickly
- Leverage a system or body of work that has already been created—gain exposure

LINE 5—HERETIC A.K.A. DISRUPTER

There are times when there is a need to disrupt the way things have always been done in order to make way for something better.

Affirmation: I am a force for change in the world when in congruence with my journey. I allow myself to be seen slowly over time. I fearlessly challenge the status quo. I innovate, empower, and transform. I am consistently communicating my purpose and the work I am here to do so that I attract those who will see me for who I am and the gifts that I bring. I build my inner circle slowly over time. It is safe for me to be seen when I am clear with what I am willing to fight for. I am here to lead and fearlessly share my mission with the world when I am called. I am private and therefore mindful of what I share with my followers. I showcase the highest potential for humanity and inspire with my vulnerability.

The Disrupter

Profiles include 2/5, 3/5, 5/1, 5/2.

As a fifth line disrupter (also known as the heretic), you are a tremendous power for change and good in the world. You can influence (and seduce) others into new ideas and inspiration. With this great power comes great responsibility to influence for the greater good.

You are destined to help others. Your energy is magnetic and influential, and it is not simply through your actions that you influence others. You are a mirror for others energetically. This mirror helps others to get congruent with their design and healing. While you might not consciously be aware of this, your energy does this simply by existing. This makes it difficult for people to see who you really are.

The fifth line is a projected profile, so others will project onto you their expectations. Others will call you in when all of the regular ways of doing things have failed, and you will be asked to save the day, create change, and help others transform. It is important that when answering these calls, you decern whether this is correct for you. Is this truly something *you* want to come in and disrupt?

When you are "saving the day" on all the right disruptions, you can amass a big following. You are influential, transformative, healing, and empowering. You will constantly be influencing people in the right place and at the right time when you follow your strategy and authority.

Communicating for the disruptor is very important. This communication is more effective when done in a deliberate, repetitive, and concise way. It's important for you to be very clear in your message. Since others don't always see you for who you are. Making sure you are clear in your message and knowing who you are is important for the fifth line.

The disrupter can be a master of hiding since from a very early age people have been projecting onto you *their* expectations. This can be very trying for the disruptor. You can often feel like no one truly knows who you are even when you've been clear and vulnerable with them. This can lead you to come across as private to others, but it is simply because you have been projected on and you play your cards close to your chest as a result.

In close relationships, it is important for you to move slowly and build trust over time. This slow, deliberate, clearly communicated process of building a relationship will support you in ensuring that you are building trust in a way that is healthy for you. As you build trust with your inner circle and in your close relationships over time, you will slowly reveal your true and authentic self. You bring a magic energy and spark to your relationships. They evolve, thrive, and grow like an ecosystem. The disruptor will always seek the highest expression of love in their close relationships.

You are here to disrupt the status quo—a force for change when all else fails. People turn to you when they have tried all the normal ways of doing things and are ready to try something new, innovative, outside the box.

You embody the highest level of expression within your chart—you have a depth about you that can seem to be endless. You have the capacity to influence a massive number of people. You enchant, entice, and magnetize people to you with your personality, ideas, and presence.

As a result of the projection field, the disruptor needs time to recharge and reset from the projections of others. Your retreat time allows you to answer the next call when it comes. It is important to honor this downtime. This ebb and flow of calls will happen throughout your life. You are not meant to always be fighting, disrupting, and living in the projection field. In fact, you magnetize more people to you when you retreat for a bit and then reemerge refueled.

You are here to create an impact in the world for the greater good of humanity. Spend time getting to know yourself in order to live your purpose. Get clear on your values, mission, and what is worth fighting for. The more you know yourself, the less resistance you will face with projections. When you clearly communicate who you are and what you stand for, even though you truly never share it all, the sliver that you do share will magnetize the correct people to you. You have big things to do in the world, and while you may feel like hiding, it is important for you to answer the calls that are in congruence with your design. The world needs you.

Line 5—Distilled
- Universalizing, Projection, The General
- Step in when all the standard solutions fail
- Often invite in people in need or people in crisis to project onto them a potential for rescue

- Get others to see the potential power that is there
- Must be mindful of what others see in them that might not be there or expectations that they cannot meet
- Are sometimes private due to the projections they face
- Take time to establish trust and safety in relationships
- Have a dichotomous relationship with the world in that they want to be seen but like to hide
- Must become truly self-aware of who they are to avoid the projections of others
- Can be seen as the someone who saves the day (projections)
- Must be on standby and ready when crises may arrive

LINE 6—ROLE MODEL
A.K.A. MENTOR

There is beauty in individuality: the nuances that make us each unique color the diverse tapestry that is the core of the human experience.

Affirmation: I am the hawk that flies above, the one who climbs to the top of the mountain. I see from a higher perspective. I am here to show others how to be their authentic and unique selves by being a living breathing example of embodying my own uniqueness. I embrace the three phases of my journey, which teach me to grow my wings and ultimately soar above. I am a living example of how when you embody your individuality, you can fly; in fact, you are meant to. Every step of my journey brought me to embodying more of myself, to growing my confidence when the time comes so I can take flight. I fearlessly take flight with confidence and soar above while following my journey. I land in an effort to usher others into flight as well so that we can all fly if we want to, showing others we are each unique, authentic, and special.

The Mentor

P rofiles include 3/6, 4/6, 6/2, 6/3.

The Line 6 is here be an example to show us how to live out our lives as the best, most individual version of ourselves. As a Line 6 or a mentor you are not wondering whether other people's gardens are better than yours, you are simply worried about making sure your garden is the most vibrant, brilliant, unique, beautiful expression it can be.

The mentor or role model (as it's known in the Human Design System) is here to be a living breathing example of what it means to be an individual. You are here to be of counsel and provide an unbiased opinion. You are wise, grounded, and comfortable with yourself once you are in the third phase of the sixth line. You are a master of your life.

The mentor has three distinct phases to their profiles that you will go through as you age. This is different from the other profiles. The first phase of the mentor (from birth to around thirty years old) is similar to that of a third line. You are here to experiment and experience. You may hit road bumps along the way, and this can be a challenging time for the mentor.

During the second phase (from around thirty to around fifty), the sixth line is healing from all the bumps and bruises of their first thirty years. This is often a period of retreat and studying others. Some sixth lines may even think they are depressed during this phase. It is during this time you may find certain activities take more energy than they used to. You may also notice a softening of the sharp edginess you had/experienced during your twenties.

Part of this phase is focusing on yourself and your business. Getting clear on what you like and dislike, your purpose in life—this is the phase where you do the work. In doing this work, you gain more clarity on what it means to be you. It is during this time the mentor really begins to step into their own, and as a result, their confidence soars. You become keenly aware of yourself and slowly become a master of your individuality.

It is during phase 3 (from roughly fifty years old) where you synthesize the phase 1 experiences of your life as wisdom with the mastery and inner work of phase 2 to move into your true calling as a role model. It is not unusual for a sixth line to have dramatic changes during this time because you desire to live a life that is in congruence with your authentic self. You will want to experience your authentic self in all areas of your life.

It is during this time that you step into your true calling. You have had many experiences, and those experiences have given you the wisdom to discern what works and what doesn't, and you are now living as your unique and authentic self.

Most sixth lines are clear on their purpose, and if you are not, your outer reality will make it abundantly clear and push to get the attention for you to live in congruence with your Human Design. If you are out of congruence with your design, you will struggle to get out in the world and will appear almost aloof.

As a mentor, you embody your role by standing in your own unique truth. It is through standing in your uniqueness and individuality that you inspire others to do the same. You truly want to show others how to fly. You want them to feel what it means to soar, and you know that does not lessen who you are. You know that the more of us who can fly, the better off we will all be. You don't have to do anything to stand in your mentor role. Simply by existing you are a mentor and role model to others.

Line 6—Distilled

- Administrator, Optimist, Peacemaker, Mentor.
- Are much like an eagle or hawk soaring above—perspective.
- Experience three distinct stages of life:
  - Stage 1—Birth to thirty years: Much like a third line, exploring and living life through trial and error—Can adopt a pessimistic view.
  - Stage 2—Thirty to fifty years: Time of retreat and inner healing. Take their bird's-eye view to determine what really works and develop resources. Begin to step into their wisdom and become a role model.
  - Stage 3—About fifty years: Encouraged to fully engage with life and the world as the more optimistic and authentic self. Radical shifts may occur at this stage. The role model is awakened.
- Live their unique purpose, and in doing so, inspire others to do the same.
- Live by example—lead by leading.
- Are deeply trusting beings and model to us how to live our own unique life.

AUTHORITY OVERVIEW

I n the Human Design world, you will often hear the advice "Follow your strategy and authority." Strategy is how you are designed to interact with the world, and authority is your decision-making process. The reason you hear "Follow your strategy and authority" is this is the foundation of keeping your life in flow and living with ease. When you follow your strategy, which is tied to your type and then your authority, you will be met with much less resistance in life, or dare I even say, more flow and joy.

The challenge with following your authority in general is that so many of us are conditioned to rely on the head (and others) to make decisions for us. The goal for the head is to use that thinking in service of others and rely on our own strategy and authority for the decisions we make. The challenge is the head is loud and convincing. It is the not-self spokesperson for all of the centers. If you have a head that is defined or undefined, it can still be conditioned, and on top of all of that, the head is a pressure center. The pressure to know. We are conditioned from a very early age to seek the approval of others, often betraying our own inner knowing. A big part of living your design and tuning up the definition in your life is learning to calm the head for yourself and lean into your strategy and authority.

For me, and to continue with the lighthouse metaphor, strategy and authority is the beam of the lighthouse calling you back home again and again. It is beckoning you, encouraging you, quietly reheading you. If you follow your strategy and authority, you will always find your way home again. It is in the following of this strategy and authority that you will always be able to find your way back to yourself again no matter how far out to sea you go. The more you connect with your strategy and authority, the easier it will become to access it.

Let me give you an example: as a Projector, my strategy is to wait for the invitation and my authority is emotional. For me, flow and ease look like waiting for the invitation while I ride my emotional wave and get to an emotional neutral before making a decision.

In my opinion, many of the Human Design resources out there don't go deep enough in providing support with authority. To me, honoring your authority is one of the key aspects to living a life in high definition. When you fail to make decisions in a way that is congruent with your design, you will most certainly be met with major resistance along the way.

For some of you, your strategy and authority may be the same. Take, for example, a Generator who has sacral authority. This Generator with sacral authority can make decision in the here and now and trust that is the right decision for them. Now a Generator with an emotional authority cannot necessarily do that, especially when it comes to big decisions in life. I will dive into more of the nuance of this later, but this is something to be mindful of.

The Hierarchy of Authority

EMOTIONAL AUTHORITY

There is beauty in riding through the waves of the storm. You experience the depth of the ocean, the crashing of the waves. The depth. The emotion. And ultimately, the glass-like calm after the storm.

Affirmation: I ride the ebbs and flows of my emotions. My clarity comes with time. I am deliberate in my decision-making process. I make decisions on my terms. I do not allow the pressure of others or our rushed society to influence me. I honor that I will never be absolute in my decisions. I move forward in action when I've gotten to an 80 percent yes or no. I ride the crashing waves and the storm of my emotions and make decisions only when the sea is calm and the fog has cleared.

Getting to an Emotional Neutral

Nearly 50 percent of the population has emotional authority. Emotional authority ordinates in the solar plexus, and when it is defined, it has precedence over all the other authorities within the Human Design blueprint. The solar plexus has four distinct emotional waves:

The Source of all Waves originates from the Channel of Mating 59-6—breaking down barriers and bonding us together in pursuit of creating new life. This is a stable wave and requires another person to bring it to life.

The Tribal Wave—Need—This wave ratchets up in three distinct notches and then explodes and resets its process over again.

- Channel 19-49
- Channel 37-40

The Individual Wave—Passion—This wave operates through moods and moodiness. It is even keel most of the time but has spikes of up and down moodiness.

- Channel 39-55
- Channel 22-12

The Collective Wave—Desire—This wave operates through desire, feelings, and experiences and has distinct peaks and valleys where its feelings may crash.

- Channel 36-35
- Channel 41-30

Determining which wave you have, and you may in fact experience multiple waves or a combination of waves, is how you can learn to embrace your emotional authority.

If you pause for a moment and think about the last decision you made from an emotionally charged place, how did it turn out? Probably not as you expected. Now think of the last time you made a decision from an emotionally neutral place. Did it work out? Likely.

The reality is when you have emotional authority, you must make your decision from an emotional neutral. With emotional authority, it is important to note a few things:

1. Eighty Percent Is a Decision—You will never have 100 percent belief or buy-in that a decision is for you. For example, if you get to 80 percent, that is a yes (or a no) for you.

2. Clarity Comes Over Time—You must make your decisions from an emotional neutral. Never a high or a low. The amount of time it takes to get to this emotional neutral will vary from person to person.

3. Integrate Your Strategy—You must take into account your strategy. This is where it gets challenging especially for Generators, Manifestors, and Manifesting Generators (more on this later).

Let's first talk about coming to an 80 percent decision. I know, as someone who has emotional authority, I have on many occasions (before learning about my authority I oscillated back and forth in my decision-making in part because I was never 100 percent. I would have a decision to about 80 percent, and then ultimately, I would let my head talk me out of it with a *Yeah but. . . what about this and that and the other?*

The reality is, as someone with emotional authority, my 80 percent decided is the decision for me, even if it seems counterintuitive or like in my case where the "Yeah, but" of the head took over and convinced me otherwise. Ultimately, it took me far too long waffling back and forth, causing myself more pain along the way (in true Line 3 fashion) in my indecision.

For many of us with emotional authority, especially as we begin to tap into it, it's important to set some guidelines for ourselves on how long we will be "undecided" before we take action. The reality is with emotional authority combined with the not-self of the head, we can stay in indecision for weeks, months, or even years because we aren't 100 percent convinced the decision is right for us. Learning to embrace that when we get to 80 percent that is the correct-for-us decision and then moving forward is an art.

The second part of emotional authority is that clarity comes through the passing of time. It is not in the here and the now. When you have emotional authority, there is no instantaneous decision. You ride your emotional wave, and once you have arrived at an emotional neutral, your clarity comes. The length of time varies from person to person, so getting to know your wave is part of the process. For some, it may simply require sleeping on it, while for others, it may take a few days or a week.

Then, of course, consider and align with your strategy. This is especially important for Manifestors, Manifesting Generators, and Generators who have emotional authority. I find this can add a layer of complexity to their process.

For Manifestors, this can look like having an initiation and then pausing to ride their emotional wave (waiting a day or two), and then once they get to a neutral, if that initiation is still a yes for them, then they move forward with informing the key parties.

For Generators, this can look like having something to respond to or be lit up by (the Generator strategy), riding their emotional wave, and then tapping back into their sacral response to confirm their decision.

For Manifesting Generators, this can look like visualizing the outcome they want to achieve, waiting for something to respond to, riding their emotional wave, tapping back into their sacral response once some time has passed, and then informing (assuming it is a yes for them).

I have witnessed far too many Manifestors, Generators, and Manifesting Generators who have failed to honor their emotional authority who ultimately end up in situations that have created major resistance and tension in their relationships. This often leads to drama and regret in their own lives because they failed to ride their emotional wave.

Projectors with emotional authority who can seem "hard to get" may find themselves even more magnetic to others. The energy they create by asking someone to let them "sleep on it for a few days" can come across as elusive and therefore, it creates more of an invitation from others. As a Projector with this authority, be sure that the invitation and recognition is correct for you and you aren't simply settling for the first invitation that came along.

Emotional authority is very nuanced, and it is important for all types with this authority to get to an emotional neutral before coming to a conclusion. For some of the types, this may be a challenge because you feel a strong urge to move; trust me, ride the emotional wave. Leverage the energy to work on something small when it comes to making the decisions, or do something entirely different to burn off that energy. Waiting is critical for the emotional wave because clarity comes over time. There is no knowing in the now with the emotional wave.

SACRAL AUTHORITY

There is no need to wait, for the clarity you are seeking is in the here and now. Its truth bursts up from within the body, guiding the way.

Affirmation: I trust the inner knowing that comes from within. It lights a fire within my body, and I can feel it— the inner pulling or pushing, the instantaneous yes and no that bubble up from below. My answers are here in the now. The clarity I seek comes from within. I trust it. I honor it. It is the light that will guide the way, illuminating my path step by step.

Recognizing the Sacral Response

With sacral authority, the person will have a defined sacral. This occurs in Generators and Manifesting Generators who will also have an undefined solar plexus (emotional authority trumps sacral authority). The sacral provides answers in the here and now.

Sacral authority is the feeling of being lit up from the inside, especially when something is a yes. The sacral, when asked yes or no questions, responds with "uh-huh" or "ut-huh" sounds. Children with sacral authority are a great example of this, especially before conditioning from adults sets in and they are told to "use their words." The sacral response of this authority doesn't come from the head, and in its truest expression, it is the sounds, not the yes and no.

It will come from within, typically from the diaphragm area of the body. I have on many occasions witnessed those with a sacral authority while on Zoom calls physically move closer to the camera or further away depending upon whether something resonates for them.

Sacral authority originates in the sacral, and it is experienced by many as a full body response. You will experience a fire from within. Open-ended questions are the enemy of sacral authority. The best way to tap into this sacral response is with yes and no questions from a trusted advisor.

My youngest son is a Generator, and when we ask him a yes or no question, you can see the amazing power of the sacral. It takes over his body and pushes and pulls it. I remember I was asking him whether he wanted mac and cheese for lunch while he was in the midst of playing LEGO, and before he even knew what was happening, he was pulling away from me with his head shaking no. The words and sounds of the response came moments later.

Some of you might be thinking, *Well, I don't feel that body response*. This is often as a result of conditioning since many of us are taught at an early age to "use your words." Learning to tap back into that sacral response becomes really important. I always recommend starting small and calming the head as the head is typically the one that takes over the decision-making. Have someone ask you questions that you already know the answers to and see what bubbles up. You can also have someone ask you really polarizing questions. For example, if your least favorite food was broccoli, you could have someone ask you whether you like broccoli. Reconnecting with the sacral response takes time. You must rebuild your trust with that "in the now" response without letting the head override.

SPLENIC AUTHORITY

There is wisdom in that inner nudge that says, "Do this, not that." Its subtle whisper contains the wisdom of a thousand lives keeping your heart beating and your soul alive.

Affirmation: My body is present and grounded in the now. I listen for the subtle nudge, the whisper in the ear, the inner knowing that ushers me forward. It carries the wisdom of one thousand years, and I trust in its wisdom even when it makes no sense.

The Inner Nudge of the Spleen

Those with splenic authority will have an undefined sacral *and* an undefined solar plexus. This authority derives from the spleen, which is the oldest of the centers and carries the primal wisdom of survival. This center is intuitive and is concerned with the survival of the species.

With splenic authority, the subtle nudges within the moment to moment are where clarity whispers. Splenic authority is this inner gut knowing that something resonates or doesn't. It's walking into a restaurant and simply knowing that it's not a good idea to eat here tonight. It is that inner response in the moment that can be trusted since it is based on survival. Some say it whispers and only speaks once, while others say it will speak twice.

From my experience, it can be a subtle but inner nagging, a gut feeling that seemingly comes out of nowhere. You can trust this feeling. I suggest that if you have this authority, play around with it. Many people with this authority often remark, "I was supposed to go to dinner at this place, and I later learned a bunch of people got sick there" or the same with a natural disaster: "I was supposed to be there, but for some reason, I chose not to go." While these are bigger examples, this is the type of feeling that one with splenic authority will experience with decisions big and small.

Since the spleen is concerned with keeping you safe and alive, it is important to learn to trust this response. This center is easily overwritten by the demands of the head center and the pressures of others, which may cause you to second-guess your splenic wisdom.

HEART AUTHORITY (EGO)

There is beauty in following through on your commitments when your heart is in it. Honor the tension that exists between work, play, and rest.

Affirmation: I only commit to actions if my heart is in it. The heart works so that it can play. I tune into the desires and yearning of my heart and fearlessly follow through. If my heart's not in it, I gracefully decline. I work, I play, and I rest. I honor the tension and dichotomy of these energies to keep me fueled. I dance with life's ebbs and flows and the seasons of life while only committing to what my heart truly desires.

Getting to Know Thy Heart

There are two different types of heart authority. The first is heart center manifested authority; only Manifestors will have this authority, and it is a direct connection between the heart center and the throat with no other centers defined. The second is heart center projected authority; only a few Projectors will have this authority, and it is a direct connection between the heart and the identity center via channel 25-51.

Couple of things to note: before I distill the differences, with either type of authority (and for anyone with a defined heart), this center stays healthy by making and keeping commitments, especially to oneself. You will lose your connection to your defined heart if you fail to follow through on your commitments. The heart has the will to power through and complete what it starts. In order to discern which commitments are a good use of your energy, be sure "your heart is in it," especially when the energy commitment is over long periods of time or it's a big commitment.

The defined heart works so that it has time to play, so finding the balance between work and play for anyone with this authority or a defined heart is critical. The defined heart craves work, play, and rest on both an energetic and physical level.

Heart Center Manifested Authority

With heart center manifested authority, it's all about the ability to articulate and manifest. This authority is expressed verbally through the throat from the heart via channel 45-21. If you have this authority, both your heart and throat will be defined, and you will have the complete 45-21 channel with no other authority centers colored in. Manifestors are the only ones who can have this authority.

With this authority, it is all about what you actually say in the moment. This authority is clear when you are blurting out what you say rather than scripting out what you think you should say.

The impact and truth of this authority reside in what you say in the moment, trusting your voice and the words that come out of your mouth without your head overriding. The truth of your voice is the initiator, the trusted source, and it will lead the way. Someone with this authority has a great deal of open centers, so staying connected to your voice is key to being connected to your authority. Do not let the not-self of the head override. Trust in your voice and let it guide you.

Heart Center Projected Authority

The heart centered projected authority is a rare form of Projector where they will have no other defined centers except for the heart to the identity center via the channel 25-51. It is especially important for these humans to follow their strategy and authority by waiting for the invitation and then selfishly asking themselves, "Do I want to do this?" or "What will I get out of this?" or "What is in this for me?"

Since this authority is derived from the heart, which is the will center of the body, understanding what the benefit is to you is important since the will center will have the energy or not to follow through. If your heart is not in it, it is not a correct invitation for you. This type of Projector has powerful and potent leadership when they are being invited and then being selfish in their decision-making style by getting clear on what the benefit is to them.

While you wait for invitations, it is important for this authority to learn about the systems on which you will be guiding others. Since the authority lacks a connection to the throat, having people around you to invite you is important. Understanding the not-self of the many undefined centers in your chart is also critical. With a powerful defined identity center connected to the heart, you have the power to follow through when you are invited and your heart is in it.

SELF-PROJECTED AUTHORITY

There is truth in listening to my voice. It brings me closer to myself and the highest expression of myself. My voice shines light on my direction.

Affirmation: I listen to and trust my voice and the words that come from within me. I hear them. They are my truth. They guide me to the highest expression of authentic and unique self. I listen to my words as they reveal the wisdom of what will bring me joy. I let go of overthinking and trust that the words that bubble up from within are what will guide me in the correct direction while simultaneously giving me more and more clarity on my individuality.

Learning to Listen to Your Own Voice

This authority originates through one of four channels where the identity center is connected to the throat. Someone with this authority will have a great deal of openness in their chart, and letting go of conditioning and the not-self of all the open centers will be important for this type of authority.

With this authority, your clarity comes when you talk it out and listen to the words that you have to say. It is in this talking it out that you will hear what is best for you. The important thing to understand with this authority is to listen without letting the head get involved. It is in the listening of the words that you are saying where clarity and decisions are found.

This authority will have no motors found within their chart. People with this authority can very easily get lost in the flood of information coming in to them via their open centers. Learning to embrace instead of ignore their voice is fundamental for them to live in congruence with their strategy and authority. It is in this listening to their voice that they will find true happiness and fulfillment. With a defined identity center connected to the throat, you are designed to be guided by what makes you feel like the truest expression of yourself. Does this bring me joy? Will this decision make me happy? Does this bring me closer to feeling like myself? Is this in congruence with who I am?

This authority will often find themselves as a great guide for others. Remember: you must ignore the head and its nagging. Listen to what you have to say without thinking or dissecting it. Simply listen and you will find your truth.

ENVIRONMENTAL AUTHORITY

There is a place where clarity comes. Peace finds you. The decision arrives. This place is sacred. Find Yours.

Affirmation: The world around me unlocks my path to success. This world is sacred. It is mine. It brings me peace and keeps me grounded. I honor the wisdom it provides me, and I listen intently to what it is saying to me. I relentlessly cultivate it so that we both thrive. I ruminate and then decide.

Listening to Your Environment

Environmental authority is only found in Projectors, and it is a rare authority. This authority only occurs when the ajna is connected to the throat, or when the head is connected to the ajna, or when the head, ajna, and throat are connected. No other defined centers will be present for this authority.

This authority is guided by the environment they are in. This design takes in sensory information from the world around them via the open centers they have. Then they discern by feeling whether this is the correct environment, people, and idea for them. This authority often asks, "Is this the right place or environment for me?"

While it is helpful for you to have trusted advisors, it is important not to rely on them or the head to intervene in your process. It will often be helpful for those with this authority to ruminate on their decisions with the intent of getting out of their own body and leveraging the advisors as a sounding board in order for the environmental Projector to hear what they have to say.

With all of the openness in a chart with this authority, it is critical to avoid the head stepping in and taking over with decision-making. If you have environmental authority, it can be helpful to you to actually visit the place you are potentially making a decision about. You may also find that you have a place, potentially in nature, that is supportive to you in processing your decision since you must take in sensory information from the environment in order to gain clarity.

LUNAR AUTHORITY (REFLECTORS)

There is a world around me that reflects the answers I seek if I know where to look. I trust the world to spark my sense and give me clarity.

Affirmation: I trust that the clarity I seek comes with the passing of time. The world around me mirrors back to me the answer I am searching for. With each day that passes, clarity comes. I trust in the world around me because I've carefully curated it. I seek out my trusted advisors to listen to my contemplations without the need for them to respond. My knowing will arrive in the discussion I create.

Waiting Twenty-Eight Days

With lunar authority, there are no defined centers. The only type with lunar authority is a Reflector. Their strategy and authority is to wait twenty-eight days. It is during this time where the moon will go through the sixty-four gates of the transits that Reflectors with lunar authority get clarity.

There are two key factors for those with lunar authority: the first is their environment and the second is having a set of trusted advisors to talk it out with. Reflectors are a mirror of the community and people around them. Therefore, their environment is incredibly important to them. This environment will act as a mirror reflecting back to them. If the environment is not right, the lunar authority will not come to the right decision.

Reflectors also need to have a group of trusted advisors with whom they can talk it out. They need to have conversations and dialogues to gain clarity as they listen to themselves. Then one day, during the twenty-eight day cycle, they will simply come to a conclusion and inner knowing based on their conversations.

DEFINITION OVERVIEW

When it comes to definition in a chart, it is important to note that in some charts, there may be separate and distinct areas that are defined. This is not good or bad; it simply means that you will not have access to all your defined energy within your chart when you are on your own. Throughout your life, you will seek to bridge the missing half of the gate or the channel within your chart.

This is where the energetics of others come into play to help you bridge the flow gaps in your chart. I will share more about this later; however, I find that it is important to shine awareness on this at this point since in the next lesson we will be getting into the centers. The split in definition tends to become more prominent as we get into that content.

With any splits in definition, it will often present itself in your life as something missing or something wrong with you. It is, in fact, quite the opposite. You are whole as you are. This electromagnetic bridge is simply a magnet for the people you will attract into your life. When you have a missing gate or channel, you will attract people to you who have that "missing energy." When this happens, be sure to follow your strategy and authority to ensure it is the correct-for-you person to have in your life. You will often be able to find a lot of wisdom in the gate where there is a bridge within your chart. It is important to recognize that this energy is not yours (the bridge gate or channel) and learn to discern when you are in the not-self of this energy.

Some of you with split definition may, in fact, feel two very different energies all within yourself, but you may struggle to access them both at the same time. Or you may find that when someone in your house is home vs. not home, you may have different energetics. This is likely because this person bridges the splits within your chart. While I truly believe you don't need to actually be in the physical presence of the person, you might find when you are around certain people, the energy is quite magical for you both. This is likely because they bridge an energetic gap within your chart. This happens without you having to place much thought into it. In fact, if you pull the charts of the people within your inner circle, you will likely have people in there that already bridge the gaps in your "missing energy."

Breaks in flow within your chart via the gates and channels are areas that are subject to conditioning just like the undefined centers within the chart. This may lead you into the not-self and convince you to fill the void of the missing pieces within your chart. We may observe this energy as "What is the problem with that person?" when in reality it is often something we have been conditioned on within ourselves.

In the business world, I often recommend pulling the charts of the key people in your organization, simply because people can present as the not-self themes and present an energy that is not theirs. To ensure that there is an electromagnetic match and people to bridge the gaps in your energy, I pull the chart. Of course, please get permission before doing so.

Understanding your definition is incredibly important, especially in terms of making decisions; however, your strategy and authority always take higher priority than your definition. If you have a split in your chart and a big decision to make, often spending time in a public place alone can help you process or get clear. Ultimately though, your strategy and authority are there to take precedence and guide you to be in congruence with your higher purpose.

Definitions Distilled

No Definition—There are no channels or centers defined within the chart. This will only happen in a Reflector.

Single—There is a single area of definition where all the channels and defined centers are connected within the chart. The energy flows without a break in the areas that are defined. People with a single definition have an ever present, consistent, continuous, and reliable energy. They do not need others in order to feel a sense of wholeness or to process information. They will often digest information very quickly unless they are emotionally defined. People with a single definition are self-contained.

Split—There are two separate areas of definition, channels, and centers within the chart that can be connected with a single gate (although there may be more than one area where this connection can happen). These people will often experience the not-self of the bridge gate that they do not have in their chart. It is important to get familiar with that energy in order to discern what is actually yours. This bridge gate will often be subject to a high level of conditioning in your chart, more than your undefined centers.

Wide Split—There are two separate areas of definition, channels, and defined centers that cannot be connected by a single gate. They need a channel and/or multiple channels and centers to be connected. The channel or channels where there is a wide split will be the area with the greatest conditioning within the chart. This will often present itself as "It's not me; it's the other person" in an almost victim-like way. Conversely, there is often great wisdom to be found in this area as well when the person is in congruence with their strategy and authority.

Triple Split—There are three distinct and separate areas of definition within the chart that are not connected to one another. These people will have several bridges in order to connect the flow of energy in their chart. With a triple split, these people often experience more conditioning through their open centers than in the bridge gates in their charts. While it is still important to understand and know the energy of the bridge, the not-self of the centers is often more prevalent. Triple splits are often impatient and can act prematurely; however, they are often also driven, ambitious, and assertive. It is healthy for people with triple split definition to interact with many different people on any given day, which helps them to get their energy to flow. They will often begin to feel suffocated and trapped if they are only around one person.

Quad Split—There are four separate areas of definition within the chart that are not connected to one another. People with a quad split will have eight or nine of the centers defined within their charts. The bridge gates or channels will take precedence in terms of conditioning and not-self followed by the undefined center within their chart. With a quad split, these people have a lot of set ways in their being due to all the definition within their chart. They may be or seem to be difficult, inflexible, or challenging. They are simply slower in their decision-making process, and if they are forced to comply with the expectations of others on how fast they "should" move, it can be incredibly destructive to their being. Quad splits need time to make their decisions because they have to process all the information through the many different areas of definition in their charts.

THE CENTERS

As we dive into the centers, I think one of the most fundamental things to remember about the centers is the themes. Centers are a key component in the Human Design chart. When we begin to understand the themes of each of the centers, we can then have a baseline understanding of what the person in front of us might be experiencing without having to even look at the gates.

Memorizing the themes is key to mastery in Human Design. The themes of the centers give life to the conditioning that someone may have taken on. The gates give awareness to the energy that is present (or not) with the person in front of us. When we look at the center, we must look to both the themes and gates, but also to the person sitting in front of us. Their experiences. Their culture. Their age. Their upbringing. Their career. Their community. It is not just about the chart. It is about the whole person, the pieces of the chart, the synthesis of how the chart comes together, and the recurring themes you see in the chart. It is no one thing. It is all the parts that make up the whole. The pieces of Human Design cannot exist without the whole. I encourage you to keep this in mind.

As you enter into your own experiment and support others with theirs, I recommend holding space for yourself and the other. The centers, in particular, are a place where deep memories, layers of conditioning, and potential trauma are stored. This is a place to tread lightly and honor the depth the person in front of you desires to go.

When you get into centers work with people, it is about first creating awareness. Without awareness, depth, conditioning, and integration never happen.

First we must educate, shine a light on what the center means, what its high and low expression is. How it is coming to light in yourself or the person in front of you. We each have our own unique language we use to express our thoughts, experiences, and opinions. The language we choose is going to be different for each person, so listening for the keywords of the themes of the centers is key.

When we think about the centers and the conditioning that takes place within each center, we must also take into account that in undefined centers, we may have a tendency to overcompensate in the gate that we don't have. I often hear people say, "I don't relate to that." Then I will offer up the opposite side of the gate and the person relates. This is because there is a break in the flow of energy. We overcompensate for the energy that we don't have. This is one of the places where definition comes into play.

For split definition, triple split, and quad split, the gate will often carry conditioning. Now I don't want to go down the rabbit hole of this in the centers section, but I want to plant the seed of this here because as we look at the chart and the centers within the chart, I want you to have an awareness of what may be coming up for people.

Centers Overview

In Human Design, there are nine centers within the chart. Each center has meaning, definition, personality, and flow. It is through this definition or openness that the lens through which we see the world is brought to life.

When we have definition in our charts (the colored-in areas), there is a sense of knowing. These areas are fixed and will be with you throughout your life. These are the areas where we become more of who we are. There is a set personality built into these areas of definition.

Think of the child who craves patterns at age five and insists that all the bottles in the refrigerator point out; they will only crave that need for order more at seventy-five. It is within us, built into who we are. However, we can cut off access to our definition and live in polarity of that center.

When the centers are white in the chart, this means they are undefined with gates coming off of them or open no gates at all. These areas have no fixed or set personality. The gates coming off of the undefined center will provide some flavor, but it is ultimately a filter or a place where you can try on different outfits. It is in these undefined or open centers where we can get into the not-self because we can't regularly access the energy here and have no fixed personality.

These are places where we can take on conditioning. The energy is inconsistent and unreliable, but these are the centers that pull us into life. This is where you learn lessons, carry baggage, and filter through your experiences to determine what is truly yours. Think of these areas as places you can go shopping to try on what might work for your style.

The struggle or challenge is conditioning. We take on "stuff" from others, unknowingly—"the shoulds." We carry baggage from our parents, our friends, our family, our culture, our mentors, and our coaches, even our past. This baggage contorts our true essence. It makes us jaded. It cultivates incongruencies. It clouds our decision-making. It leads us off of our paths and the impact we are here to make. It leads us to the not-self.

When we are in the not-self, our mind is the spokesperson. It takes over. It plants seeds of doubt even though we know something is right for us. It spreads fear when compassion is needed. It keeps pushing us forward when we know we need to rest. It overwhelms us with emotion. It leaves us feeling unworthy or not enough. It creates resistance and has a sandpaper effect everywhere it goes. This is the not-self.

The reality is it is impossible to escape the not-self. It is part of the journey. A learning and discerning of what is truly ours and what is that of the other. When we can get to know this "not-self" is when our world can change. It's about bringing awareness to it and shining a light on what the not-self sounds like, how it erupts in our world, and how to wrangle it as life evolves. The ability to manage ourselves widens.

We become more capable (and have more awareness). We stay in our bodies more. We find more happiness, peace, and joy. We are present. We find more understanding and empathy for others. We embody what it means to be human by living in congruence with who we are meant to be.

It is important to note that all of the energy in the chart flows to come out of the throat. Dive into the workbook for more information on the centers and their themes.

HEAD CENTER

There is knowledge hidden as deep as the ocean if we would only open our minds and curiosity enough to see it. This knowledge is around us, waiting to be unlocked through each encounter we experience with one another.

Affirmation: I honor the pressure to know. It does not define me. It lives beside me. It brings depth to my understanding, creativity, knowledge, and consciousness. I know I must not act on my pressure to know; it is simply there to provide knowing. It is in this knowing I find solace, allowing my doubt, worry, and anxiety to pass through me like the sound of the wind passing through a field. I am not the pressure to know.

The Pressure to Know

Head Center—Pressure Center—Mental pressure, inspiration, questions, doubts.

We will start our journey with the head center—this is one of two pressure centers in the body (the other is the root). The head is the source of the pressure "to know." The head is here to provide us with wisdom and be a source of guidance for *others.*

The head is *not here* to make decisions or worry itself with directing our day-to-day lives. The head is a pressure center that moves energy toward awareness. The head feels pressure to know, understand, and comprehend things in the world.

Simply put, the head is here to ask questions and expect answers. The head is one of the trickiest centers in the body to master (for a plethora of reasons). We are taught from a very young age to think, which ultimately disconnects us from our body's inner knowing and immediately gets us into the logic, creativity, and thinking of the mind. The head craves knowing; it is literally the pressure to know. The head questions why; it inspires, it ideates, and it conceptualizes. The head is the source of questions, confusion, and doubt, especially when it creeps into our decision-making and how we interact with the world.

The reality is the head is not here to be a decision-making tool for our lives. The head is intended to be in service of others, not ourselves. But we often default to our head or mind for our decision-making, for making sense of things. This is because the head, in conjunction with the ajna, which together are known as the mind, is the not-self spokesperson for all the undefined centers in our bodies. If we are in our mind, we are in the not-self of whatever particular center we are having doubts around.

Getting to know the not-self of the head is critical to letting go of what is not yours as the mind (head and ajna operating together) is the not-self spokesperson for all the undefined or open centers in the chart. Simply put, the head wants to tell you what to do. It likes to tell us what we should say and what we should do. It craves making decisions, and it is here to offer wisdom for others, not decisions. Recognizing the not-self monologue is key to becoming congruent with your design.

The pressure of the head is not here to drive action; it is here to drive mental activity. The head in simple terms is ask questions, expect answers.

The head has three gates coming off of it that direct our thinking:

- Gate 63 is focused on securing the future—"What."
- Gate 61 is focused on the present—processing new information in the moment and discerning whether it is worth pondering "Why."
- Gate 64 is focused on making sense of the past—"How."

The head is an incredible source of wonder and awe in the body. It has the incredible gift of knowing the unknowable. When healthy, it is a powerful source of creativity.

In the body, the head center is associated with the pineal gland, which regulates the flow of information between the gray areas of the brain and the neocortex.

The Defined Head: 30 Percent of the Population

With a defined head, there is a set and fixed way of thinking based on which channel is activated and connected to the ajna. There is a constant mental pressure to know and seek answers. The mental pressure of the defined mind can heighten mental anxiety, especially with what it has yet to grasp and gain a full understanding of.

Since the defined head and defined ajna (if you have a defined head, you will have a defined ajna since there are only three channels coming off of the head), you will feel pressure to take action on your thoughts. Neither the head nor the ajna are motor centers. Taking action on your thinking will only result in being out of congruence with your strategy and authority. You will also feel pressure to share the questions, ideas, and inspirations you have. Again, rely on your strategy and authority to ensure you are waiting for the right time to bring these into the world.

The Strengths of a Defined Head

- Tend to be clear and set on what you believe
- Have consistent access to your thinking
- Are a well of knowledge and ideas
- Have a fixed process for discerning questions and answers

The Challenges of a Defined Head

- Default to negative thinking
- Struggle to stop thinking
- Have limited bandwidth in terms of your thinking
- Struggle to get out of your head and into your body
- Struggle with acting on your thoughts
- May not always be right (even though your head thinks otherwise)
- Struggle to manage the near constant mental activity

Action Tips for a Defined Head

- Use meditation as a tool to occupy the mind
- Give your mind a job to do vs. worrying about making decisions for you
- Use inquiry and recurring questions to gain clarity from the defined mind
- Come to peace with mental pressure as it is part of your life
- Understand that patience is important
- Rely on your strategy and authority for decision-making
- Know that your thoughts are a catalyst for thinking, not for taking action

The Undefined Head: 70 Percent of the Population

The majority of us have an undefined head or mind. The undefined head is a great source of wisdom when used for the right purposes. The challenge is that many of us are relying on our undefined heads for decision-making. This is not correct. With an undefined head, you are a filter; you amplify the ideas and thoughts of those around you. Thoughts, ideas, and inspiration flow through you. Flow being the key word.

Many people hold on to the thoughts, ideas, and inspiration that come into the undefined head. They identify with them, become them, and ultimately consume them. The mental pressure from the world around them takes over their mental monologue, and they end up in the not-self of the head. Anxiety and the not-self set in, and the mind becomes conditioned.

With an undefined head, people either avoid intellectual pursuits or they immerse themselves into them, seeking to be the one with the most knowledge since the head is the pressure to know. With an undefined head, it is easy to get caught up in problem-solving, overthinking, anxiety, overwhelm, and indecision—the pressure to answer the questions of others and consume more and more information.

The undefined head is here to be a filter. It is here to be an observer—detached from the thoughts that it experiences/that flow through it. The healthy undefined head is here to explore the wonder and curiosity of the world, of life, and our consciousness. With an undefined head, you are a reflection of the thoughts of those around you, while sprinkling in new insights and observations.

A healthy undefined head discerns which ideas and contemplations are worthy and which are not. The healthy undefined head offers up new insights, ideas, and inspiration for others. It is filled with intellectual possibilities on all subjects. It is open to the beauty and depth of the unknown and allows doubt and confusion to pass through. It relies on its strategy and authority for its decisions and allows the mind the beauty of deep inquiry for others.

The Strengths of an Undefined Head
- Can be flexible and fluid in your thinking
- Absorb people and information on a deep level
- Have the possibility of a still mind—when healthy
- Possess deep wisdom and the potential for great expansion
- Live in wonder and awe about the human experience
- Capable of depth of thinking

The Challenges of an Undefined Head
- Don't rely on your mind, especially for decisions
- Struggle to remember things
- Prone to the mind becoming easily conditioned
- Under constant pressure to come up with answers
- Struggle to create boundaries around consumption of content
- Struggle with anxiety
- Can feel like "there's something wrong with you" and have a need to prove one's intelligence
- Can be easily overstimulated by too much information
- Tend to think about things that don't matter

Action Tips for an Undefined Head
- Learn to tolerate mental pressure without the need to take action
- Become an observer of your thoughts without them becoming part of your identity—you are not your thoughts
- Lean on your strategy and authority for decision-making
- Mediation and practices that ground you in your body
- Be mindful of what you consume—set clear boundaries, especially with social media and any other content that can induce the not-self of the mind

The Not-Self of the Head

The mind is the not-self spokesperson for *all* the undefined centers within the Human Design chart. Becoming aware of this not-self talk is the key to deconditioning the not-self and getting back in congruence with your Human Design blueprint.

The not-self monologue of the head sounds like…

- I need to be inspired. Let's go here to get inspired.
- I have lots of questions . . . I need answers to these questions.
- Who has answers to my questions?
- I've got to find more answers; who has answers to my questions?
- I should know/have a better understanding of this by now. What is wrong with me?
- Why can't I remember?
- I need to make sense of . . .
- If I just keep looking, I will find an answer/understanding/inspiration/idea.
- Where can I go or who can I talk to, to find answers?
- Is this supposed to be interesting?
- Am I interesting?
- What am I supposed to be thinking about?
- How am I going to figure this out?
- What am I going to do?
- Why can't I find answers?

The Gates of the Head

If you would like to dig deeper into the high and low expression of the gates, please download the book workbook at www.humandesignforbusinessbook.com.

- Gate 64—The Dreamer: I support you in making sense of the past by visually finding patterns in the world. I answer the question "How does this all make sense?"
- Gate 61—The Truth Seeker: I support you in contemplating "the why" of the present to spark creative inspiration. I answer the question "Why did this happen?" in order to be a catalyst for an epiphany.

- Gate 63—The Inquisitor: I support you in spotting the logic and patterns of what might emerge in the future. I answer the question "What do we need to be mindful of in the future?"

The Head Center in Biz & the Real World

When it comes to the head center, I see so many themes over and over again where this center keeps entrepreneurs especially stuck, overwhelmed by all there is to learn. I see this appear over and over again as a result of boundless social media consumption to the point of detriment. This is the center that keeps us stuck thinking, *I just need to learn one more thing. If I have that information, then I will be ready.*

This center is full of overwhelm, overthinking, and the pressure to know more than we do. This is the anxiety of not knowing something and needing to know more. This anxiety "to know" supposedly helps us understand and make sense of our lives.

Since 70 percent of the population has an undefined or open head (and since not-self themes apply to defined pressure centers), this energy stops people in their tracks. It keeps them from moving forward. It leads them to believe that they do not know enough. That they "need" more and more information.

The head center instills doubt and leaves people wondering whether they "know enough" or have enough information. They then compare their progress to the progress of others via consumption. This energy is reading a book and then looking up the other books recommended while in the midst of reading the book. This is the energy of stalking a competitor on Instagram and thinking they know more than you do.

The head center leaves us overwhelmed with inspiration and again leaves us feeling like we don't know which idea to pursue. This overwhelm of inspiration keeps us frozen and stuck because we struggle to discern via the mind which idea is correct for us. This is where following strategy and authority is key because the head center is meant to be in service of others, not for ourselves. But the head longs to be in charge since it has been for so long. This pressure keeps people overthinking what to post, what offer to pursue, or how to structure their programs, offering, or business. This energy is the pressure of *too* much. Too much consumption, too many ideas, too many questions and things to find answers for.

In defined head centers, this energy is often in a state of overwhelm, but because they only have one fixed way of processing the questions, answers, and inspiration in the head center, they often struggle to be coached or supported. With a defined head, there is always a fixed mental pressure in the body (vs. the undefined or open head that can be calmed). This fixed mental pressure is something that the defined head must learn to live with.

The fixedness of the defined head center may come across as "uncoachable." They only see things through the lens of their definition. They will struggle to put their mental pressure into the shoes of how someone else may experience it. They may struggle to do meditative work and calm their mind. They have to learn to dance with the pressure they experience and manage it. It is and will be ever present. *So* the question becomes, how do I learn to live with this mental pressure of needing to know more?

With a defined head, the person will have a defined ajna as well. This means a fixed way of taking the knowledge and processing it in the ajna. They have no ability to oscillate between the different channels or gates. Whatever is activated in their chart is what they will have to work with. This is not good or bad; this is simply what they must work with.

With this knowledge, you can then support them better based on their fixed way of seeing things. This might mean that if you don't present things in the way that "makes sense" to them, they may not "get it." This is often simply because of their configuration. Look to the channels that are present—is it the gate of the past (how), the present (why), or the future (what)?

With a defined head, the question becomes how do I contend with the mental pressure that I feel in order to relieve (even momentarily) the mental pressure I feel. For some, I have seen singing and dancing working well, short guided meditations of under five minutes, and setting intentions when going for a walk. For example, "On this walk I am going to let go of my mental pressure to _____." However, the reality is this is something that they must live with. The challenge really becomes how can I use my mental pressure in service of others? How can I quiet my mind?

With an undefined head, the gates that they have present will help anchor their energy; however, they can still oscillate between the different energies since they are taking in the energy of the defined heads and amplifying it. It is also important to consider your own head gates (or channels) here when working with clients with open or undefined head centers. How do my presence and energy support them in thinking in a different way? Do I open up any new ways of thinking for them?

The undefined head and open head are ones that love to consume. This is the ability to binge-watch TV and endlessly consume content for hours on social media. The undefined (or open head) has no fixed way of asking questions or seeking answers. They will simply have a bit of energy that grounds them in what's theirs based on their gate or gates.

This may appear as the person who buys all the books and never finishes them. This is the person who overthinks what to post and then never posts. This is the person who is constantly under pressure for inspiration and information. The open head in particular is often curious while also confused because they have no set way to process.

The undefined and open head can be zen once they reckon with amplifying the pressure of the defined head. This means coming to the realization that the mental pressure that they feel to consume is not theirs. Practices that calm the mind are very helpful because with an undefined (or open) head, we must release the pressure of the head in order to calm it. This could be setting time limits about what and who you consume information from. The not-self of this undefined (and open) center can be really negative and all-consuming, so carefully curating what you consume becomes key. Setting clear boundaries around content consumption is also imperative. Pair those boundaries with practices that calm the active mind, and you can begin to access the wisdom and depth of an undefined or open head.

It is important to note that since the undefined and open center is the not-self spokesperson for all the centers, it can be tricky to peel back the layers of conditioning brought about in this center. It is twofold because the mind wants to be in charge. It was in charge, and now its purpose has changed. It is here to be in service of others, not for ourselves. This is coupled with the fact that our society puts recognition and praise on our minds and our thinking. Getting to the root of the conditioning at this center is not for the faint of heart. The not-self of this center tricks you into checking boxes, leading you to think you are ticking boxes when, in fact, you are crossing stuff off your list from the mental pressure.

AJNA CENTER

There is clarity in awareness of the knowledge that surrounds me. I use the thoughts, insights, creativity, and opinions in pursuit of the greater good, my bigger purpose.

Affirmation: I value my ability to process the world around me. It is perfectly designed for me and my purpose here in the world. I embody the knowledge and use it in service of others. I honor my depth of knowledge wherever it lies. I am present. I am grounded. I honor my strategy and authority while knowing my thinking is the spark in the world for those that surround me.

The Source of Mental Awareness

Ajna Center—Awareness Center—Consciousness, conceptualization, thoughts, insights, opinions.

The ajna is one of three awareness centers in the body. It is the only awareness center in the body that does not have access to a motor since it is placed between the head (pressure center) and the throat (manifestation center).

The ajna is much like an interpreter taking inspiration/ideas from the head and turning them into useful information for review, research, and ultimately, communication. Think of the ajna as a processing hub. This is where you process information and prepare it for communication/manifestation in the throat. This center makes sense of the inspiration from the head. It can see the whole and all the different parts simultaneously. The ajna is the capacity to differentiate, discern, and analyze. In short, it is here to do research.

The ajna is the source of our consciousness, conceptualization, thoughts, insights, opinions, and mental anxiety. The ajna creates awareness around our perception via two processes, one visual and one acoustic. The visual process is concerned with what has been and what might be, while the acoustic is associated with pure inspiration and the pressure to know now.

Mental awareness was the second awareness to evolve, and it is the predominant way we view our world. We are taught from a very early age to rely on our thoughts and our logical way of thinking. The awareness derived in this center is one that can have a long shelf life—a lifetime. For example, when you make a decision from the not-self, the mind (head and ajna combined) can replay this decision over and over again for the rest of our lives. With each replay, it will come up with another opinion or suggestion as an option to try. It will be a source of endless options to try. You get stuck in a cycle of suggestions and dead ends. None of these options are correct though since the mind is not here to make decisions. Recognizing this cycle and that the mind is meant to be in service of others is key to breaking free. Shining awareness on this cycle of opinions, options, and dead ends of the ajna is key to getting yourself out of confusion and disappointment.

The ajna processes information in a this or that way. It weighs two or more options simultaneously. It can look at both the positives and negatives and construct arguments for both sides that oppose one another. This is why this center is so tricky to work with because it can convince you either or. Remember the logical ajna is not here to make decisions; it is here to simply process information. It will help make clear how many sides there are to consider, but it cannot be trusted to make decisions.

The ajna provides us with analytical gifts and is fundamentally dualistic. It presents both or many sides to every argument. It will hold truth to both sides.

We cannot know our truth or what is correct for us from the mental rationalization and comparison. We must rely on our strategy and authority to guide us to what is best for us at the correct time.

When we create awareness, it is the result of having successfully dealt with fear, or in the ajna, it often appears as mental anxiety. We must confront this mental anxiety in order to live in a healthy way with this center. In the ajna, this is often the fear of not knowing or of the fear of being misunderstood.

The value of this center comes from our mental intelligence and our ability to share and empower others with our unique perspectives when they are in congruence with our strategy and authority. We are here to have encounters with one another, articulate the human experience, enrich the lives of others, store information for future generations, and contemplate the wonder and awe of life's possibilities.

When we are in our thoughts, our body is often tense or rigid. When we grab onto our thoughts, there is tension in our body because the brain is occupied and not fully present in the moment; therefore, we do not have the full ability of our intellect in the moment.

A healthy ajna is open to what is arising and flexible. It is truly the ultimate witnessing observer. It is a brilliant mechanism to build a community and empowers through its multiple perspectives and possibilities seen from a place of clarity and unattachment. With a healthy brain, you have the ability to reverse action, meaning you are not caught in a loop or pattern in the brain. If you get attached to a belief or to being right, you can get in these loops—which are unhealthy *if* you cannot get out of the loop. I will share more on this in the defined and undefined sections.

The Defined Ajna: 47 Percent of the Population

There are six gates coming off of the ajna. With a defined ajna, you will have consistent access to your information processing centers. Which channels you have will determine how you process information.

The Head to the Ajna—The head to ajna connection (the mind) will be constantly active, processing the information it provided via the channel defined.

• Channel 64-47—Right brain/abstract information

- Channel 63-4—Left brain/logical information
- Channel 61-24—Innate inner knowing

The Ajna to the Throat—The ajna to throat connection will have consistent access to speaking your mind.

- Channel 17-62—Acceptance—in touch with your opinions and share them freely (left brain)
- Channel 43-23—Structuring—working to articulate your unique insights in a way they can be understood (inner knowing)
- Channel 11-56—Curiosity—compelled to form your multitude of ideas into stories to share with humanity (right brain)

With either iteration of this definition, you will have mental preference and a tendency to think in a certain way depending upon the channel activations within your chart. With this center defined, you will always be thinking about and processing information, being creative, and influencing others.

If you have a defined ajna, you can become dependent on your mind for decision-making, and it can often logic you out of your authority. This is not correct for you. It is important to use your ajna in service of others and rely on your strategy and authority for decision-making.

The Strengths of a Defined Ajna

- Can trust your mind—you have a stable mind
- Inspire others
- Designed to be certain which can be grounding
- Rely on your mind to hold and process information
- Enjoy/love mental stimulation
- Have a strong mental ground—not easily swayed or influenced by others

The Challenges of a Defined Ajna

- Have a constantly active mind
- Struggle with mental anxiety

- Can be overwhelmed by the pressure to know from the mind
- Struggle to believe your thinking, therefore, overriding your strategy and authority
- Have the potential to be certain or fixed in your thinking
- Can be inflexible and headstrong
- Feel inadequate if you are unable to put your thoughts into action
- Struggle with timing
- Can become dependent on your ajna for your sole source of wisdom
- Must learn to honor the timing of your information—one person's poison is another's medicine—must understand whether the person is receptive to your knowledge

Action Tips for an Ajna
- Learn to embrace the active mind instead of resisting it
- Value your certainty while leaving space for not being correct
- Train yourself to receive information, analyze, and then turn to your authority for your decision-making
- Work with your timing
- Be present
- Get to know the gates you are working with
- Detach from your thinking

The Undefined Ajna: 53 Percent of the Population
If you have an undefined ajna, you have a very fluid and free way of thinking. If your ajna is undefined, so is your head. With this combination, you have an open mind. This is often a sign of mental intelligence and a sign of a free thinker, once the mind is set free from conditioning.

With an undefined ajna, you have no fixed way of thinking; therefore, you don't hold on to concepts, ideas, or opinions as the only truth. You simply won't identify with any one thing. You can contemplate deeply and discover the world through your intellectual gifts.

Those with an undefined ajna have the capacity to sift through the myriad of ideas and possibilities and discern which concepts have value. Those with this configuration can often pick up on ideas before anyone else when in a group setting.

The challenge with the undefined ajna center is that it is often conditioned from a very early age, and it is put in a box, especially in a school setting where children are pressured to think in a certain way.

With the undefined ajna, your ideas can come out of nowhere and can be incorrect or irrelevant. This often leads you to stop sharing your insights because you don't want to "look stupid."

If you learn to discern that the mental pressure to think in a certain way is not yours, the ajna can become a playground that can provide a depth of wisdom for others. The gate coming off of the ajna may have some influence on how you "think" as with all of the undefined centers.

The Strengths of an Undefined Ajna

- Can be wise and discerning about which information is worth processing
- Process information in multiple ways
- Flexible in the ways and lens you look at life
- Can have a photographic memory
- Tend to be a brilliant thinker
- Mentally stable

The Challenges of an Undefined Ajna

- Tend to have no consistent way of thinking or processing information
- Struggle to hold on to thoughts, ideas, and information
- Can appear ungrounded mentally
- Struggle to focus
- Can feel uncertain
- Can appear aloof because you are afraid to share
- Prone to comparing yourself to others
- Can get caught up in the details

Action Tips for an Undefined Ajna

- Learn to clear the conditioning of the ajna—meditation and therapy
- Become a witness to your thoughts (detach from your thoughts) to find

grounding and stability
- Use essential oils to help change state
- Practice breathwork
- Practice somatic work of getting in the body

The Not-Self of the Ajna

As with all the centers, the head is the not-self spokesperson. The not-self mental monologue of the ajna sounds like . . .

- I have to figure this out.
- What should I do with my life?
- I must be able to figure this out on my own.
- I can't share that idea; they might think I'm stupid/silly/weird/a freak.
- What's my next move?
- I'm certain that _____.
- I have to "know" the answers.
- I'm not going to share my opinion/ideas/thoughts because I don't want to be challenged.
- I have to be ready for a challenge and to defend my ideas.
- What am I going to say?
- I have to put my life in order to get rid of this chaos.
- I have to make this new idea a reality.
- Where is my next move?

The Gates of the Ajna

If you would like to dig deeper into the high and low expression of the gates, please download the book resource at www.humandesignforbusinessbook.com

- Gate 47—The Aha Moment Stimulus: I support you in seeing the possibilities and solutions. I answer the question, "How can I expand?"
- Gate 24—The Explainer: I support you in making sense of the past and rationalizing. I answer the question, "Do you have an explanation for _____?"

- Gate 4—The Service Provider: I support you with my ability to always have an answer (even though it may not always be correct). I answer the question "Ask me anything. I have an answer."
- Gate 17—The Farsighted Pathfinder: I support you in seeing the many different paths/strategies there are to get to where you want to go. I answer the question "What is the best way for me to get to x?"
- Gate 43—The Insightful Genius: I support you in having an insight that is "out of the blue" or unexpected. I answer the question "What needs to be healed, reckoned with, or tended to in order for me to have a breakthrough?"
- Gate 11—The Idea Generator: I support you in coming up with ideas. I answer the question "I don't know what to do next/pursue next. Which idea is optimal for me to pursue?"

The Ajna Center in Biz & the Real World

The ajna in business often presents itself as the mental anxiety of being misunderstood by others and/or not being able to communicate with clarity to others. The ajna center differs from the head in that the head is the mental pressure of not knowing, while the ajna convinces us "we won't be understood" or "we can't clearly communicate our message."

In entrepreneurs, I see this as the overwhelm and overthinking of what business model to commit to or what to post on social media, and the struggle to have others "get their way of doing things." This happens in the overthinking, overcompensating, overideaing, overcommunicating, or overexplaining. Or conversely, it is the inability to communicate.

The anxieties of the ajna are as follows:

- Gate 47—Uselessness, failure, meaningless
- Gate 24—Inexperience, naivety, ignorance
- Gate 4—Chaos, turmoil, confusion
- Gate 17—Challenge, defiance, opposition
- Gate 43—Rejection, ignored, dismissed
- Gate 11—Gloom, lack/block, hopelessness

With a defined ajna, at its lowest expression I see this emerge as being uncoachable and very rigid. There is definiteness that is present in the defined ajna, but the question becomes how do you use this fixedness to your advantage? How can you leverage it as a superpower instead of a rigidity? It is the inability to see things from another person's perspective. It is a fixed way of thinking and processing things. It is a near constant mental anxiety that you must learn to contend with and manage.

The defined ajna is not a curse, in fact, quite the opposite. The challenge is learning to contend with its fixedness, moving from this inflexibility, rigidity, and inability to be vulnerable to using the superpowers of your fixed ways of processing things. It's important to learn to dance with that rigidity and realize that with a defined ajna, your way of researching and processing information is not the only way. When those with a defined ajna can embody that, at its highest expression, the defined ajna is a reliable source of reaching, processing, and communicating our sensemaking with others.

For entrepreneurs with a defined ajna, this can appear as being stubborn, being unwilling to negotiate, having to be right, or wanting to be the last one to speak, or conversely, it can provide others a consistent way to look at the world and process information.

For example, I have the 17-62 channel defined. This gives me a very consistent way of oscillating between big-picture thinking, understanding all the details, pathways, and strategies, and recognizing (and naming) things that may come up along the way. I use this in my business in service of others to help them get to where they want to be in life and business. People can rely on this fixed way of thinking in their chart to tap into this gift of thirty thousand-foot thinking and one thousand-foot thinking and everything in between.

With an undefined ajna, there is no set way of thinking. It is fluid, and it can access all the different energies of the gates in the ajna, which also means it can access all the anxieties of the ajna.

People with an undefined ajna, especially entrepreneurs, have a well of information available to them, but then can't always access it on demand. It ebbs and flows.

When someone with a undefined or open ajna is present with those who are defined, they can move from logical fixed thinking if the person has the channel

17-62, or if they are in the presence of someone with the channel 23-43, they may be very artistic in their process.

The anxieties they experience are rooted in the gates that are present in their chart. Any of the other anxieties they experience are the ones that they are amplifying from the people around them. They can let those anxieties pass through them.

In my experience of supporting clients with an undefined ajna, I have to be very mindful of what I bring to the table in terms of my own ajna while giving them space for their process, which can present as very all over the place. It moves from abstract to logical to visual and back again. They may even lose their train of thought mid-sentence, and this is normal. They may also offer up incredible insights out of nowhere.

At its lowest expression, the undefined or open ajna presents as the person who cycles around and around, never truly making progress. They bounce from idea to idea, never really committing. They often become very overwhelmed and end up frozen, struggling to decide what to do, and swinging from one extreme of knowing to not knowing, overcommitting to not committing, overcommunicating to not communicating, having tons of ideas to no ideas.

They swing on the extremes, ultimately never committing to one path of moving forward. They want to do all the things but fear none of them will work nor do they know how to communicate what they want to do.

At its highest expression, people with an undefined ajna allow the amplified energies of others to pass through them, and it provides them with a well of ways to think, to reason, to make sense of things. These people often have incredible insights and open up new ways for people to see things. They show us a new way to think; they are creative, insightful, and a well of inspiration (and wisdom) for the world when they regularly get clear on the energy that is theirs in this center.

Clearing the filter of this center and really learning to lean into the fluidity of thinking is key. Practices like meditation where you can calm the mind are key. An undefined ajna has the ability to be calm and free from mental anxiety. Whereas the defined ajna does not have this luxury. The defined ajna must learn to contend with the ever present mental pressure.

The undefined ajna must be tended to. Journaling, singing, and recognizing which anxieties are yours and which are not yours becomes the key. Become an observer of the anxiety that you experience. When you experience a certain anxiety, is it due in part to who you are around? Do you always experience the same mental anxieties with the same people? Look at the charts of the people in your life (with their permission, of course) and see how their energy may be impacting you. This will give you insights into what energy is yours and what you can let go of. The Hawaiian Ho'oponopono is an excellent exercise to do when you are experiencing mental anxiety.

Remember, both the head center and the ajna were formally what kept us alive before we transformed from seven centered beings to nine centered beings in 1781. This evolution gave us more consciousness. The transition gave our mind and ajna new roles. It transformed us from a species concerned only with survival to a more highly evolved species who had opinions, insights, ideas, and consciousness. This new role of the head and ajna is here to be in service of others, yet the head and ajna want to be in charge of us. This is why we "should" ourselves, why we "logic" ourselves, instead of relying on our strategy and authority.

THROAT CENTER

The voice gives life to our inner beings, our self-expression, our impact, and what we long to create in this world. It is through our voice we connect, we share, and we express our unique individuality in the world.

Affirmation: I trust in my ability to give life to my thoughts, feelings, intuition, and ideas in the world. I honor the divine timing as I bring my words into the world and share them with others. I value this unique gift as it transforms and interacts with the environment around me. It is my unique configuration that gives substance to my self-expression. I use my voice as a powerful voice for creation, transformation, and impact in the world.

The Manifestation of Communication, Transformation, and Interaction with the World

Throat Center—Manifestation Center—Intuition, instincts, fears, body, awareness, immune system, time.

The throat center is where all the energy in the Human Design chart wants to come to fruition in order to create and manifest. All of the energy in every center in the body wants to make its way out of the body through the throat center. If you were to think of the Human Design chart as a town, the throat center is the town square.

The throat is the one manifestation center in the body. It is where all energy is flowing and under pressure to communicate and act. The throat is the most complex center in the body. It is how we express ourselves. It is how we manifest our life's purpose. It has a splendor to the magnificence it can create.

The throat creates. It creates our relationships, creativity, survival, well-being, sense of self, and power. The throat gives voice to our thoughts and words to our feelings, and it allows us share our intuitions. We use our voice to lead and influence, share, create, and connect with others. It is where we put our energy into words, then our words into action as we create. This center is filled with possibility and creativity.

Your capacity to show up, be heard, create, and manifest rests in your relationship with the throat center. It has a huge impact on the human experience.

In the body, the throat center is associated with the thyroid and parathyroid glands. The thyroid oversees the metabolic processes in the body.

The throat is primarily focused on communication, expressing who we are and what we are feeling, and creating learning, sharing what we know, what we want to contribute, what we have seen or heard, and what we can contribute to empower others.

There are eleven gates coming off of the throat center that give life to our communication style. These are sometimes referred to as the voices of the throat center. These gates will set the stage, and depending on what is activated in your chart, the style with which you will communicate. Your voice will come from the gates and channels activated coming off of the throat center.

- Gate 62—I think
- Gate 23—I know
- Gate 56—I believe
- Gate 35—I feel
- Gate 12—I try
- Gate 33—I remember

- Gate 8—I can
- Gate 31—I lead
- Gate 20—I am
- Gate 16—I experiment

It is through these activations that you will have consistent and reliable access to your voice. This center allows us to communicate. The ability to communicate effectively ensures the quality of our relationships and ultimately our survival.

It is the throat center's job to make our unique selves known to others in unique ways so they can interact with what we are saying and what we will ultimately end up doing. This communication shows us what is viable before taking action (as well as what's not viable).

Words and communication give life to our truths. Learning to dance with our strategy for guidance and our authority at the correct time is critical for this center. Whether this center is defined or undefined, it is imperative to follow your strategy and authority. This center is under tremendous pressure to speak and to do; however, when working with this center, timing is critical. Too soon or too late and the communication will not be received. Getting to know the gates you have and those subject to amplification is important for using this center in congruence with our unique design.

This allows us to engage with others in the correct ways that are also fulfilling to our being and our purpose. We trust and wait for the correct time based on our strategy and authority.

The throat's secondary function is manifestation as action or doing. Those with a motor connected to the throat (Manifestors and Manifesting Generators) can set things into motion and bring to completion what they envision.

The Defined Throat: 72 Percent of the Population

With a defined throat, your throat center acts as an energy hub for all of the messages coming in through the different centers in the body. These messages are then communicated through the eleven different gates of the throat and manifest as communication and action.

The healthy throat is a reliable source of definition. The throat can express or act from six different centers.

- The heart speaks from the "I"; for example, "I want that, I have that, I will do that"—take leadership.
- The ajna speaks what the mind is thinking and conceptualizing—speak your mind.
- The solar plexus speaks or acts on the emotions or feelings—express your feelings.
- The spleen speaks spontaneously, intuitively, and knowingly in the moment—speak your intuition.
- The sacral speaks through the responsive sounds of the sacral in the moment—manifest your action through words.
- The identity speaks from personal identity, self-expression, and direction from the higher self—make a unique creative contribution.

The defined throat is a consistent, reliable but limited way to express itself.

The Strengths of a Defined Throat

- Have consistent access to your voice
- Have a certain level of confidence in expressing yourself
- Tend to honor your type, strategy, and authority to better empower your voice
- Give your defined throat a voice—put it to work for you

The Challenges of a Defined Throat

- Must speak to the bandwidth of the definition you have
- Must speak with a certain tone or intonation with how you say things
- Struggle to let your voice guide your action instead of your strategy and authority
- Tend to speak without honoring the timing of your strategy or authority
- Struggle with not being heard and criticized

Action Tips for a Defined Throat
- Witness your voice and don't attach your identity to it
- Appreciate and be grateful for your gifts
- Start a journaling practice
- Creatively express yourself and experiment with this
- Take part in speaking circles

The Undefined Throat: 28 Percent of the Population

With an undefined throat, you have a sophistication with your voice that is invaluable. You have the capacity to tune into another person and meet them with your voice. It is a powerful force. You have deep flexibility and fluidity spanning the tone of your voice to the content of what you say. You have the potential to access any of the channels driving the throat.

The challenge with an undefined throat is that you are amplifying the pressure to speak of 72 percent of the population. Those with an undefined throat can often feel pressured to speak and speak more than those with a defined throat. Or conversely, they can become fearful of opening their mouths, feeling out of control in that they don't know what will come out when they speak. You may even feel unable to communicate effectively. With an unhealthy throat, you will often talk too much or not at all.

Learning to rely on and gain confidence in your strategy and authority to guide your communications is important when you have an undefined throat. You may also find you spend a lot of mental energy on thinking about what you are going to say next, only to be surprised by what actually comes out. This is the challenge of an undefined throat.

The Strengths of an Undefined Throat
- Have endless possibilities in the voice of the undefined throat
- Voices can flow freely and show up in a variety of different ways
- Can be the spokesperson for a group since you amplify the energy
- Can be a magnet for others
- The gates ground your vocal power

The Challenges of an Undefined Throat

- Struggle with speaking but not being heard or noticed
- Feel lots of pressure to talk but don't know what to say
- Can use up your energy trying to think of what to say and/or to be seen or heard
- Tend to blurt things out
- Prone to talking too much
- Struggle with planning what to say
- Depend on others to manifest

Action Tips for an Undefined Throat

- Become skillful with your timing
- Become an observer of your voice
- Relax, trust, and stop trying to control
- Take part in speaking circles
- Express yourself creatively through play and other creative outlets

The Not-Self of the Throat

As always, the mind is the not-self spokesperson for the throat. Becoming aware of this conditioning is important to noticing when the throat is in the not-self. When the throat is being represented by the mental monologue or soapbox of the mind, it sounds like . . .

- Look at me! Pay attention to me.
- Is anyone here noticing me? Listening to me?
- How can I get more attention?
- I feel invisible.
- Where can I go to get the attention I want or deserve?
- What should I do or what should I take action on?
- What will I become in life?
- This silence is making me uncomfortable. I better say something.
- I better initiate this conversation so I can be heard.
- I better say something because no one else will.

- If I say this, will I finally be noticed?
- How come no one is recognizing me?

The Gates of the Throat

- Gate 62—The Abstract Communicator: I support you by providing certainty, naming, and details of what might emerge on the path. I answer the question "Could you explain _____? This is where I want to understand/go/learn more about."
- Gate 23—The Alchemist: I support you by providing individual insights and breakthroughs, and I inject new ways of thinking. I answer the question "Which insight/innovation is worth bringing to life?"
- Gate 56—The Wandering Storyteller: I support you by sharing my stories in order to prove a point or illustrate a concept. I answer the question "What story do I need to hear in order to see more possibility, growth, or evolution?"
- Gate 35—The Adventure Seeker: I support you by sharing my vast web of experiences in order for you to gain wisdom. I answer the question "I have all these options. Which one do you think is optimal for me based on your experiences?"
- Gate 12—The Poet—Author: I support you with my power to change the way you understand the world through my transformative words and timing. I answer the question "What perception do I have that may need to be changed?"
- Gate 16—The Sprezzatura (Effortless Mastery): I support you in getting into action to gain experience so that you can become an expert/master. I answer the question "What is optimal for me to experiment with next?"
- Gate 20—The Divine Timing: I support you best when I practice what I preach. I answer the questions "What makes me a unique individual? What am I talented at?"
- Gate 31—The Reluctant Leader: I support you by being of service and listening to the needs of my community and using my influence when the time is correct. I answer the question "How can I achieve my goals?"
- Gate 8—The Publicist: I support you by promoting, marketing, and articulating what is unique. I answer the questions "How can I promote/market/get press for this? What makes this unique?"

- Gate 33—The Elder/Old Soul: I support you with my ability to listen to your story and find power in the pain that you have experienced. I answer the questions "All of this has happened. Can you help me make sense of it? What story do I need to hear? What lesson do I need to learn?"

- Gate 45—The Material Wielder: I support you by better understanding how to manage and be more efficient with your resources. I answer the question "How can we do this more efficiently?"

The Throat Center in Biz & the Real World

The throat center is the source of where we make our mark in the world. It is how we express ourselves and the individuality we bring to the table. Our voice is what differentiates us from other mammals. It is how we build relationships, create connection, and express ourselves. The throat is a manifestation center—the manifestation of our words and the manifestation of our actions.

The throat is akin to the city center of the Human Design chart. It is where all energy wants to emerge in the body to express itself verbally or through action in the body. It is our voice as we move about the world.

The relationship we have with this center often impacts our health, our energy, and how we break down and digest our food. This is a process of metamorphosis and transformation. This is where the initiation of transformation begins both internally and externally. This also means that any transformation in the body begins with the throat center and our ability (or not) to express ourselves.

The throat center governs our ability to speak and to get into action. If your throat center is defined, you will always be able to speak. If your throat center is defined and connected to a motor, you will always be able to do. The challenge with this defined center is learning when it is time to speak—as not everything needs to be spoken—and learning when to act or to do. People with a defined throat can almost always speak and do. The healthy expression of this center is learning when to speak and what is worth using your energy on.

When we have a healthy connection with our throat center, whether defined or undefined, we can share our authenticity, individuality, and insights/opinions with the world. The throat is how we make our mark in the world; it is how we bring to life our material world. We know when to speak, when to act, and when the timing is correct on things we love.

With a defined throat, you will notice these people have a very fixed tone to the delivery of their words. This is because of the definition that they have in their throat. With a defined throat, the tones you have available will be determined by the gates or channels you have defined.

Conversely, with an undefined throat, you will have many different tones; in fact, you can access the eleven gates of the throat, which means eleven different tones. Of course, the gates you have defined will determine the ones that show up most often.

In business, a defined throat often shows up with a consistent voice—a voice that expresses itself and can show up the same repeatedly. A defined throat is limited to the gates that are activated. The defined throat is fixed in the way that it operates, the delivery of the words, and how it expresses itself. Which gates and channels are engaged will discern what voices show up and the themes that they express, while an undefined (or open) throat may show up with multiple voices.

The undefined throat in business is an incredible voice of the people. Since an undefined throat takes in and amplifies the defined throat, those with an undefined throat can very easily articulate the values and needs of a group. The challenge with an undefined throat is that they often don't know what may come out of their mouth; they don't know which tone is going to show up or which words may pop up.

This makes it challenging for those with an undefined (or open) throat to build a trusting relationship with this center. This is where understanding your type and authority comes into play since you don't know what may erupt. These are the people who will often break the silence in a room because they feel the pressure to speak. These are also the people who will either talk a lot or have nothing to say. This is how the undefined throat operates, especially when in the not-self, in the extremes.

For those with an undefined throat, having conversations in public places will help them get their words out and express themselves. This is because they can amplify the energy of those around them and help them bridge the energy that they have present in themselves so they can express themselves.

IDENTITY (G CENTER) CENTER

There is no one like me. I am one. I am the one. The parts and pieces of me make up a greater whole. My unique configuration is part of the beautiful orchestra of the universe.

Affirmation: I am the one. Unique, beautiful, whole as I am. I value each of the unique pieces of myself that make me the person I am. I am love in human form. I radiate my individuality authentically, truthfully, and with pride. I embody what makes me unique. I value the gift I am here to share with the world. My destiny calls me. I honor this call, trusting it is destined for me. The pull or purpose comes from within. I honor this, and with each step, I become more of who I am. Connected. Whole. Loved. One with the universe.

The Source of Our Identity

dentity Center—Awareness Center—Self, purpose, direction, love.

The identity center, also known as the G center, is an awareness. This center is where our sense of self comes from, our purpose, our direction, and our source of love.

This identity center is perhaps the most remarkable in the whole body because it is central to our entire chart. This center organizes our entire chart, or another way to think of it is as the heart of our chart.

This center houses the purity of our being and is centered around unity consciousness. It does not house duality. This center draws love and beauty to it. It magnetizes what's needed for you to live in congruence with your unique configuration to it. People, work, places, and experiences. It is the essence of love, purity, and beauty.

When we are in congruence with our strategy and authority, we align with this force within ourselves, and magic happens.

When we don't know ourselves, we struggle to trust ourselves and our inner knowing. We fail to honor ourselves. We resist what flows to us. We essentially are at war with who we are meant to be and our lives.

The identity center houses the magnetic monopole—a single magnet that attracts and magnetizes life to us. It is the force that drives our lives, our direction, and our individuality as part of a greater whole. Many people think of this as our soul. It is the spark that gives us life and defines our unique selves.

This center sets the direction for your life. It is love itself. It is the sense of self-identity, love, and being lovable, and it gives direction for a greater purpose.

In the body, the identity center is associated with the liver and the blood. Liver function is responsible for the health of our blood, and blood carries nutrients and oxygen to every cell in the body.

The Defined Identity Center: 57 Percent of the Population

With a defined identity center, you have consistent access to your identity and direction in life. You have an inner knowing and a sense of who you are. You have a sense of where you are going. You are grounded in yourself.

With this center, you will often have a sense you are loved and lovable (although not all defined identity centers feel this); it comes across in your being. You look and act lovable. You will often take good care of yourself. You are not easily swayed by other people's expectations of you. You feel solid in yourself. You easily love and are loving. You walk your own path even if you perceive yourself as insecure.

The Strengths of a Defined Identity Center

- Have a solid sense of yourself
- Have a grounding in your being
- Not easily swayed by other's exceptions
- Have a steady stream of direction
- Are connected to love—either through loving others, animals, nature, or through loving yourself
- Have gifts tied to the channels

The Challenges of a Defined Identity Center

- Must learn to let others have their own path—you may believe they should follow yours
- May abandon yourself if you get off track and follow someone else's path
- Struggle to show up in your individuality
- Struggle to feel lovable
- Struggle in feeling solid and secure in who you are

Action Tips for an Identity Center

- Become aware of where you are loving and/or clear up any resistance with your stream of loving either to others or to yourself
- Be compassionate with your limitations of staying in your lane with respect to your identity and purpose
- Use journaling to support you in gaining clarity
- Practice Ho'oponopono for healing and forgiveness
- Practice letting go

The Undefined Identity Center: 43 Percent of the Population

With an undefined identity center, you are not designed to have a fixed identity. You will have no consistent access to any one identity or direction. You may find yourself to be chameleon-like—you have the ability to fit in any situation with anyone. You most likely have tried on a lot of different things or gone in many different directions.

You are almost like an actor playing different parts but leaving the role behind to move on to the next one. At times, this may leave you feeling lost or disconnected, not knowing who you are or the direction you are headed. Because of a lack of a fixed or stable identity, place becomes crucial and plays a big role in your life—where you live, the city, the house, where you sit in a restaurant. You are designed with an undefined identity center to have place play a critical factor in you "finding" a sense of stability in your being.

When you are in the wrong place, you will often find you are surrounding yourself with the wrong people. When you are in the right place, the people, direction, and connections made will be in the correct direction for you. If you are in the wrong place, everything else will be incorrect and be a source of great unhappiness. Since you are undefined in your identity, you are amplifying the identities of everyone around you—the wrong job, house, and relationships are a source of great unhappiness for those with an undefined identity center.

The good news is that those around you with a defined identity center will often have lots of ideas and suggestions, and they are eager to help. When an undefined identity center is living in congruence with their strategy and authority, they won't have to find anything themselves; in fact, they can't. Others will show up offering fresh directions and environments.

With an undefined identity center, it is important to trust that the way will be shown to you through your environment. You must be comfortable with waiting, pausing for the right way to appear. Your job becomes enjoying the people and places you encounter along the way, taking in the possibilities and different directions and experiencing the many different possibilities of love. With an undefined identity center, every next step will be revealed if you live as yourself.

With an undefined identity center, you are not meant to be doing the same thing forever. Your energy is mutative. There is no one thing that will fulfill your sense of being or your identity. It is the result of many things. Your being isn't a process of becoming per se but responding to what is in front of you. You creatively meet the world, moment to moment.

In terms of love, you don't have a stream of love sending out broadcasting signals from you, but instead you have a field of love in which love is discovered. Your path is not linear. Instead, the path and the destination are one, moment to moment meeting your responsive identity. Learning to own who you are and this ever changing identity is important. Let go of thinking you should be different. You are whole as you are.

With an undefined identity center, it is important to realize your path is to come home to yourself and realize everything you seek is already within you.

If you have an undefined identity center, you are an incredible guide. You can let go of your identity and love, and you have the innate ability to put yourself in anyone's shoes and offer loving, supportive, correct guidance. With an undefined identity center, you are here to be wise about the ways identity is expressed in others.

The Strengths of an Undefined Identity Center
- Tend to be fluid in your being
- Show a different aspect of yourself depending upon who you are with and your environment
- Have an openness and flexibility to who you are
- Wise about your direction and love
- Have a depth, variety, and richness to your life
- Love itself lies within you—you are love
- Strive to find a place that feels good
- Can choose from the buffet of life—not just one menu
- Serve as an incredible guide to others

The Challenges of an Undefined Identity Center
- Can have no clear direction in life
- Can easily get caught in the head making decisions due to lack of direction
- Tend to question whether you are lovable
- Have no stable or reliable identity
- Can be vulnerable to place
- Struggle to be understood by people with a defined identity center.
- Can wonder whether something is wrong with you
- Influenced by people with a defined identity center
- Struggle with the fear of being no one

Action Tips for an Undefined Identity Center

- Learn to discern what is yours and what belongs to other people.
- Learn that you are taking in the identities of people around you and amplifying them. You don't have a fixed identity.
- Figure out what location feels good to you—place helps stabilize your undefined identity center.
- Give yourself grace and compassion for times when you have taken on conditioning or direction from others. How could the relationship with this energy be different?
- Practice the Qigong inner smile.
- Find the right place.
- Practice Ho'oponopono.

The Not-Self of the Identity Center

The mind is the not-self spokesperson of the identity center as with all the centers. The mental monologue or soap box of the identity center sounds like . . .

- Who's going to love me?
- Where can I go to find who I am?
- Who am I?
- Who can show me?
- Where can I go to figure out my life?
- I have to figure out what I am going to do with my life . . . Where is it? Is it here? Is it there? Who can show me?
- I feel lost . . . Where can I find direction?
- How do I find love?
- Who will love me?
- Am I lovable?
- Let's go here because it will show me who I am.
- Let's go here because it will give me direction.
- If I have a relationship with this person, it will give me a sense of who I am.

CRITICAL

The Gates of the Identity Center

- Gate 10—The Individual: I support you with my own courage to love and accept myself. I accept you exactly as you are. I answer the question "What makes me unique?"
- Gate 7—The Strategic Advisor: I support you by putting myself in a role where I am your right-hand person. I answer the questions "What do I need to be mindful of up ahead? Where is there a fork in the road up ahead?"
- Gate 1—The Original: I support you by embracing my quirkiness, my artistry, and my individuality. I answer the question "What part of myself do I need to make come alive?"
- Gate 13—The Confidant: I support you by understanding what is not being said and reading between the lines. I answer the questions "What needs to come to the surface? What's not being said?"
- Gate 25—The Space Holder: I support you in finding compassion and understanding and letting go. I answer the question "What do I need to let go of in order to find solace/purpose/love/self-worth?"
- Gate 15—The Extremist: I support you with my ability to see the extremes in life and when it is time to shake things up. I answer the question "Is it time for an evolution?"
- Gate 2—The Visionary: I support you by understanding which direction is optimal for you. I answer the question "What is the correct direction for me?"
- Gate 46—The Determined: I support you in embodiment and loving your body. I answer the question "What do I need to do in order to nourish, care for, and be grounded in my body?"

The Identity Center in Biz & the Real World

When it comes to the identity center in business, this is a place where we either have clarity on our direction in our life and business or not. This is where we feel clear in our purpose, direction, and self-love or not.

Those with a defined identity center in business typically are very clear on their purpose and direction. They likely have a fixed way that they show up in the world, with their brand and style, and they are clear on what next steps they would like to take. The defined identity center often has a very clear purpose and a path for how they want to get there unlike their undefined identity center counterparts.

The defined identity center is always happy to dole out direction for others because it has an inherent need to have direction, unlike its undefined identity center counterparts. The defined identity center needs a direction, a purpose, and a plan. These are people who feel a sense of self-love and a great knowing of who they are and their place in the world. For entrepreneurs, this emerges as those with a vision and a plan for how to get to that vision. They know with great specificity where they want to end up.

Entrepreneurs with an undefined identity center are more fluid in where they want to end up. They know they want to roughly be in this area vs. a specific address. There is more flexibility to the vision of an undefined identity center than its defined counterparts. The undefined identity center can emerge as very chameleon-like, adapting to those around it. In fact, they may have a different style or purpose depending on who they are around.

For entrepreneurs with an undefined identity center, this means that environment will play a key role in their success since this influences who they are and their purpose and direction. For the undefined identity center, carefully curating and discerning your environment is key to your success. If you are in the wrong environment, you will be connected with the wrong people and go in the wrong direction. If you are in the correct environment, you will be connected with the correct people and going in the correct direction.

An undefined identity center is incredibly helpful when supporting others because it gives the person the ability to put themselves in another's shoes. The undefined identity can be a supportive guide into what might be optimal for others, but when it comes to oneself, you must remember the importance of having an environment you feel really good in. This is not just physical location but also relates to community; for example, a mastermind or group program.

The fluidity of direction with an undefined identity center can often lead an entrepreneur to feel rattled or less than because they do not have as clear of a purpose or path as their defined counterparts. It is important to be mindful of the fact that the fluidity that exists here is an important part of the journey for an undefined identity center. Embracing this fluidity supports them in their journey. This fluidity gives them the ability to experience all that life has to offer and allows them to carefully curate what is correct for them based on their strategy and authority.

HEART (EGO) CENTER

There is drive in us for more, ever present, beating over and over again. It pushes our society forward. It leaves us wanting . . . more. It is the will to win, to be the best, to prove ourselves. But we are not the sum of our achievements. We are whole as we are.

Affirmation: I honor the fact that I am worthy as I am. I am valuable. I contribute. I matter. My strategy and authority guide my commitments. I honor the pull I feel to prove myself and I watch it. Aware of my power, I use it for the greater good of the community. I honor the follow-through I have when I align with my strategy. I am whole. I am worthy. I am valuable. I am me.

The Will to Follow Through

Heart Center—Motor Center—Ego, motivation, willpower, commitment, self-worth, material world.

The heart center, also known as the ego center, is where our willpower, confidence, self-esteem, and self-worth come from. The heart center is the bedrock of society in that it fuels our will to survive in the community and thrive in the material world.

The heart has established our community and entrepreneurial way of life. It is our capacity and themes of value in terms of our contribution to the tribe or community.

The heart center is one of the four motor centers in the body. It is one of the smallest centers in the body, and it houses tremendous power.

Self-esteem is how we move with confidence in the world as a valued, contributing, healthy member of society. With self-confidence, we receive material good and support from the tribe in return. When we struggle with our self-esteem and belief in ourselves, we lack trust in ourselves and our own value—this results in losing our will to meet the many challenges of life and our capacity to follow through. The ego in a healthy state must be affirmed and reassured of the value of itself and its contribution to others. If not, it will shut down and self-esteem becomes self-loathing and ultimately self-hatred, which comes at a cost to ourselves and the community.

In our society, we have a tendency toward overachievement, often making promises we *know* we do not have the willpower to follow through on. We don't have the will to keep up. We go beyond what our bodies are capable of in order to prove our worth. Learning our mind's role in how we value ourselves is key to this center.

In the body, the heart center is associated with the stomach (gate 40), the thymus gland (gate 26), the heart (gate 21), and the gall bladder (gate 51).

The Defined Heart: 37 Percent of the Population

If you are one of the 37 percent of the population who has a defined heart, you have a superpower. You have the capacity to discern what you are going to do and follow through on doing it.

You are capable, competent, and inspiring. You like to be in control of your life and your resources—what you wear, where your work, and the demands on your time. You are clear on your own value, although you may have a tendency to overinflate it.

With this center defined, you tend to want to be your own boss. If you have a defined heart, you tend to be happiest when you are delivering goods to the community. You honor your body, needing to work and rest, and when listening to your body, you will have a keen sense of how you can best use the strength of your will center to benefit the tribe the most. You enjoy your work and contributions to providing for the tribe but enjoy being appreciated for your contribution. You are often competitive.

With a defined heart, you have consistent access to willpower. With the defined heart, you have the energy (like with all defined centers, when defined, the theme of energy is present) that is waiting to be expressed—it's just a matter of whether you are accessing and leveraging it. If you have a defined heart but are feeling less than capable, you are either burned out or not tapped into your superpowers of the heart center.

The heart center works so that it can play/rest. Learning to dance with the heart center and its need for fun and play is important. Otherwise, you will burn out. Honoring your strategy and authority when it comes to this center is especially wise.

With a defined heart center, leveraging the I, me, mine statements is key for you to express yourself. The expression of these statements allows the heart to strengthen whereas suppressing this need can be detrimental to your health. With this also comes the need to consistently prove your worth, and this comes naturally when honoring your strategy and authority.

With this center, keeping your commitment to yourself is especially important. When you make a commitment, you will have the willpower to follow through. You are building trust with yourself and this center as well as your self-esteem and self-worth. So, when you make commitments and don't follow through on them, you will lose access/connection to this center. To reestablish this connection, start by making small commitments to yourself and following through on them.

The Strengths of a Defined Heart

- Have the ability to follow through once you've decided to do something
- Value yourself and your contribution
- Are competent and inspire others
- Have special gifts depending on which gate you have (see the chart)
- Understand how this center can be leveraged in support of others

The Challenges of a Defined Heart

- Struggle with burnout
- Can easily get carried away—"too powerful"
- Struggle with the defined heart overriding strategy and authority
- Feel frustrated with others who don't have willpower like you
- Lose your connection with your heart
- Struggle to keep commitments to yourself

Action Tips for a Defined Heart

- Learn to accept your amazing superpower and be compassionate to those who are undefined in this area
- Become aware of the balance that a defined heart needs—loves to work but it works so that it can play
- Use your willpower for good
- Know your power (the gates and/or channels you have activated) and use them wisely

The Undefined Heart: 63 Percent of the Population

We live in a world that places a high value on contribution. There is a constant and consistent messaging of "We need more . . ." "We should . . ." "We could . . ." "We could be better, faster, and more successful if only we would do . . ."

If you are one of the 63 percent of the population with an undefined heart, you are likely stuck in a vicious cycle of wanting and needing more. When you fail to live up to the commitments (or expectations) that you previously made, you make more promises (often bigger) to make up for your self-deficiency, only to fail again. With each failure you feel worse, and your self-esteem continues to spiral. With an undefined heart center, overachievement compensates for the lack of will to follow through.

This often happens because you, like others with a defined heart, undervalue yourself to being with. You attempt to accomplish more than anybody else in order to prove your worth and how valuable you are. You "will" yourself into challenging situations that are impossible for you to complete.

This is further exacerbated because the undefined heart center amplifies the defined heart center, leaving those with the undefined heart center to believe they have the willpower to follow through. Meaning if you are around someone with a defined will center, you will be borrowing their willpower momentarily (or for a short period of time) only to have that willpower run out when the rubber meets the road. You will have good intentions to complete your goal, but that borrowed willpower amplified by your undefined heart will fade away leaving you feeling a sense of unworthiness for not following through again. This is very common in sales pages, workshops, etc.

The more one gets stuck in the cycle of trying to prove oneself, not following through, and then feeling the need to compensate for the lack of follow-through, the more one's self-esteem and worthiness will suffer.

Learning to honor that with an undefined heart center you have nothing to prove to yourself or others is the way. Be at peace knowing you will be guided via your strategy and authority to which commitments are correct for you. With this peace comes great wisdom and awareness and a healthy sense of self-esteem. You are aware that you do not have to compete with anyone and that your commitments are not tied to your worth. There is great wisdom underneath the conditioning of an undefined heart.

The Strengths of an Undefined Heart
- Have the ability to discern what is actually valuable to you—taking in the possibilities
- Can explore what is valuable
- Don't have to do anything in order to prove your worth
- Have the ability to differentiate who has real self-esteem and value and whose is fabricated
- Have a keen sense of who is practicing what they preach—testing the authenticity
- Value truth

The Challenges of an Undefined Heart
- Tend to question your value or worth
- Stuck in the cycle of trying to prove oneself in order to feel worthy

- Amplify the self-worth of others or lack thereof
- Feel like you have to prove yourself to others (or yourself)
- Tend to burn yourself out
- Struggle to believe that you have the capacity to follow through
- Tend to believe that your worth is tied to your contribution to the community

Action Tips for an Undefined Heart

- Understand how this center operates and what that means for you based on your unique configuration
- Know that you are worthy as you are, simply by existing
- Become an observer of your heart center instead of identifying with it
- Discover what you value
- Regularly clear the filter of your heart center

The Not-Self of the Heart

As with the other centers in the chart, the head (also referred to as the mind) is the not-self spokesperson for the undefined heart. The not-self of the heart center sounds like . . .

- If I get this thing, *this* will be the thing that changes the game for me (gives me success).
- This, if I have this, I will finally be successful.
- I've got to do this because if I don't, I won't be worthy.
- I've got to prove myself to show how valuable I am.
- I've got to be in control.
- If I do it like this and make this promise, they will finally see how valuable I am.
- They think I can do this, so I better prove to them that I can.
- I have glittery object syndrome.
- I am not a good _____ unless I prove it.
- I am unworthy. I don't feel deserving of that.
- I have to prove myself to them.

- She's doing it better than I am; I have to compete with her.
- This time it's going to be different . . . If I have _____, I know this will be "the thing" or "the time" it changes for me, and I will finally prove my worth once and for all.
- They will finally see how worthy I am.

The Gates of the Heart

- Gate 26—The Efficient Sales Person: I support you with my ability to sell anything to anyone by making it marketable. I answer the questions "How can I sell/market this with more effectiveness? What is the hook?"
- Gate 51—The Trendsetter Catalyst: I support you with my will to compete and be the first/best/market disrupter. I answer the questions "Does this challenge to the status quo innovate/disrupt? What do I need to do to be the best?"
- Gate 21—The Expert Resource Provider: I support you with my ability to control resources (particularly money, land, lifestyle) and be independent. I answer the questions "Where do I need to take more control/let go of control? How can I budget so that I can get x?"
- Gate 40—The Generous Provider: I support you with my ability to connect, support, and bring people together in community. I answer the question "How can I do this with more sustainability/congruence/alignment?"

The Heart Center in Biz & the Real World

The heart center is one of the centers concerned with direction in the world. The heart center is our willpower and our ego. While this center is small, it is mighty. It is one of the four motors in the body.

In business, the healthy expression of the defined heart comes when we understand our ability to influence others with our willpower. While "borrowing" someone else's willpower is not always a bad thing, it is imperative to understand how this presents when working with others. A healthy defined heart allows others to borrow their willpower in order for them to establish their own sense of trust in themselves. This is very powerful, but a fine line must be walked in order to do this in a way where the conditioning goes from supportive and helpful to toxic and negative.

Only 37 percent of the population has a defined heart. Those with a defined heart must ask themselves (in addition to following their authority), "Is my heart really in it?" If it is not in it, even if the authority says yes, then the task is not correct for them. The healthy defined heart has the ability to make commitments and goals and achieve them. The defined heart presents with a self-confidence and an inner knowing of "I can do this." This center and the gates of this center speak from the "I/me/my" perspective.

Those with a defined heart may love to work, but the defined heart works so that it can play. It must strike a balance between working and playing. The healthy expression of the defined heart thrives on this balance. There is a natural understanding with this center defined of when it is time to work and when it is time to play/rest.

In business, I see people healthily express their self-esteem and worth to others in the world. I've also seen those with a defined heart create, build, and cultivate thriving communities since this center is centered around the development of community and the material world.

To cultivate a healthy relationship with this center, we must understand that the "I" centricness of this center can be bruised during childhood. Many children with a defined heart center are told they are "too much," "too self-centered," and "too bossy." Their well-meaning parents often tell them to be more humble or be less over the top, and they try to teach them a lesson about being too much. This results in them often repressing the willpower and the ability to make material in this center into adulthood, and they must reconnect with this center in a healthy way. This can present in the body as an upset stomach ache or heart issue. The defined heart is stubborn and isn't easily controlled by others, which is part of the challenge in childhood, especially if one of the parents has a defined will center as well.

The low expression of this center is when people with a defined heart use their willpower over others in a negative way, which is often self-servicing and controlling in nature. The ego projects and neglects. It uses its power over others to manipulate and pressure those without a defined heart center. I've personally witnessed this over and over again behind the scenes of many launches in the online space. This can sound like . . .

- "If you don't do this, you won't be successful."
- "You will never get this chance again."
- "You must follow my way of doing things because I know best."
- "I can't believe that you can't follow through on this. It's not hard."
- "Put it on a credit card."
- "You obviously don't want success badly enough then."

The low expression of the defined heart often leaves others feeling unworthy and ashamed for them not being able to follow through, and it is very toxic. The classic example of this is the open cart/closed cart launch with the high-pressure sales tactics at the end to get people to sign up or the seminar where they "sell" a.k.a. pressure you into the next thing and a few days later you walk away wondering, *What was I thinking? Why the hell did I buy that?*

In the undefined heart, I see this emerge as the entrepreneur who overachieves. People with an undefined heart center often feel the need to prove themselves to others in order to show them they are worthy and that they too can "follow through." This pressure to have and to prove in this center can run rampant. It can sound like . . .

- "Look at what x has. I want that too."
- "Why can't I do what x has done?"
- "If they did it, I can do it too."
- "I must prove to them I am worthy/capable/able to have the same success."
- "I should be able to do this faster/better/more successfully."
- "Why can't I just be happy?"

The challenge with the undefined center is there is a pressure and an urge to take on the world and accomplish it all. Yet, people with an undefined will center do not have consistent access to willpower. They borrow it from others, then when they are no longer in that person's presence, they lose that connection to commit and to follow through.

Over and over again in the online world, this is present with people opting into programs and then never following through. Or changing business models over and over again and struggling to finish the things they start. They try to compete with the defined egos of the world, and they can't keep up. They don't need to keep up. It is unhealthy for the undefined heart to try to keep up with the defined heart centers of the world.

The undefined heart in business often presents itself as people who struggle with their self-worth, and therefore, they often undercharge. They struggle with self-confidence and often stay stuck because they don't feel ready.

The theme of the heart center is to work, support your family and community, and be rewarded for being able to contribute in a meaningful way. Understanding that with an undefined heart center, you are not here to push it forward or to will things forward with your willpower. You are worthy simply by existing. If you, like other undefined heart centers, push yourself too much, your heart, confidence, and self-worth suffer greatly. It is not uncommon for those with an undefined heart to pass away from a heart attack from an overworked heart.

The goal with an undefined heart center is to refrain from making promises. Forcing yourself to keep promises only damages your relationship with this center.

SOLAR PLEXUS CENTER

There is beauty in riding through the waves of the storm. You experience the depth of the ocean, the crashing of the waves. The depth. The emotions. And ultimately, the glass-like calm after the storm.

Affirmation: I am not the sum of my feelings. They are simply the experiences I have. They come and they go like the passing of a storm. I observe them. I honor them. I learn from them. But they are not me. They are simply how I experience the world, people, and things around me.

The Origin of all Emotion

Solar Plexus—Motor & Awareness Center—Spirit, emotional awareness, passion, desire, creativity.

The solar plexus is the source of all emotions in the body. It is both an awareness center and a motor. This center, whether defined or undefined, can be challenging to get a handle on.

As a species, this is where our feelings originate—passion, sadness, happiness, love, desire, and all the many emotions that make up the human experience. For many of us, we end up at the mercy of our emotions. They impact us without us even realizing we have a choice in how to process them. Like our thoughts that arise within us, our feelings rise up, and we are often left believing that the emotions are our own. We are our feelings. We attach to them and give them meaning. I'm happy. I'm sad. I'm angry.

The reality is you are experiencing the emotion of anger rising within. You aren't actually angry. You are experiencing anger. Learning to separate ourselves and our identity from our emotions is a critical part of the journey.

When you have a defined heart (it will be colored in brown on the chart), you can determine how you will experience and channel your emotions based on which channel is coming off of the solar plexus. Learning to ride the wave of your emotions and get to a feeling of neutrality before you make decisions will be key.

When you have an undefined heart (it will be white), you will need to learn to discern and filter out the emotions of others. You have the ability to be emotionally stable and even keeled when you put down the emotions of others that you have been carrying.

Expressing yourself through creativity, tapping into your body, and practicing meditation are all great tools for you to help to connect to this center.

This center is concerned with moving out of fear and lack and into that which we desire, or moving out of pain and into pleasure. It is a center that is filled with the many emotions that make up the human experience. It is filled with dichotomy, duality, and polarity. The ups and downs and ebbs and flows of life and all the "feelings" we experience come from the emotional solar plexus.

The solar plexus energy is creative and allows us to connect with others through "social awareness" or emotional intelligence. It is the center where poetry, revolution, romance, compassion, spirituality, moods, and spirit originate. This is the source of feelings, emotions, and our overall "feeling" of well-being and emotional clarity.

As a society, we are taught to be "be happy," and as a result, many of us often struggle with our emotions. We stuff them down and often fail to process the "feelings" we experience. This is problematic regardless of having a defined or undefined solar plexus. Learning to dance with the emotions we feel and becoming aware that we aren't our feelings is a big part of the unlearning/deconditioning process we must go through to have a healthy relationship with our solar plexus.

The solar plexus in the body is associated with the lungs, kidneys, pancreas, prostate gland, and nervous system.

The Defined Solar Plexus: 53 Percent of the Population

With a defined solar plexus, there is no truth in the now. Clarity comes and is gained over time with the understanding that there will never be 100 percent certainty. If you have a defined solar plexus, this will be your authority, as it resides at the top of the authority pyramid in the Human Design System. With a defined solar plexus, you will have "feelings" about what is correct for you or not.

With a defined solar plexus, people experience their "feelings" in waves. Which channels and gates you have activated will determine how you experience your "emotional wave." Learning to discern this emotional wave and the amount of time it takes for you to get to an emotional neutral will differ from person to person. If you have multiple gates and channels, you will have multiple waves to learn to navigate.

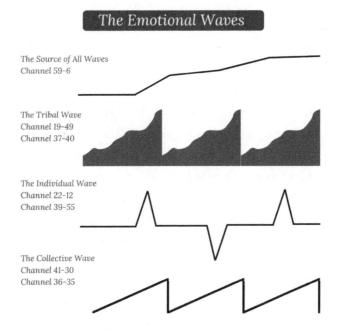

The Emotional Waves

The Source of All Waves
Channel 59-6

The Tribal Wave
Channel 19-49
Channel 37-40

The Individual Wave
Channel 22-12
Channel 39-55

The Collective Wave
Channel 41-30
Channel 36-35

There are three types of emotional waves as well as the source of all emotional waves.

The source of all emotional waves is rooted in channel 59-6. This channel connects the sacral to the solar plexus. The channel is concerned with creation, passion, desire, and needs the other in order to break down barriers and come together in intimacy. This wave is very emotionally stable, and it takes the outside influence of others to activate it.

The tribal wave, which is experienced through channel 19-49 and channel 37-40, operates through physical touch and is sensitive to the needs of others. The tribal wave is a ratcheted up, up, and up until it explodes. Part of learning to navigate this wave is learning to articulate your upsets instead of keeping them to yourself. Often these explosions could be avoided simply through touch and/or learning to thoughtfully speak your mind when you are upset. It is important to note that the source of all waves configuration will often experience their wave as a tribal wave.

The individual wave, which is experienced through channel 22-12 and channel 39-55, is often described as moodiness. I have to be in the "mood." This wave experiences smaller blips or short bursts in their waves. That said, if you have one of these channels, you will emote and you will experience the full spectrum of feelings. These channels oscillate between passionate and moody and back again. The melancholy of the lower end of this wave must be honored in order for the wave to continue flowing. There is a great deal of wisdom in the highs and lows of this wave, but you must learn to tolerate its polarity. Alone time is important for those with these channels, especially when they are experiencing melancholy. This melancholy can have a big impact on relationships, so learn to articulate to those in your life when you aren't in the mood—"It's not you. I am simply not in the mood right now." This can often dispel a lot of the tension that can erupt in relationships when this wave is present.

The collective wave, also referred to as the abstract wave, is experienced through channel 36-35 and channel 41-30. This wave has very high highs and very low lows. The low end of this wave is experienced as the world has fallen out from beneath you and often results in a crash. Lows are often experienced when expectations are not met, especially when it comes to humanity. With either of these channels, it is often important to learn to enter into new experiences simply for the love of the experience without setting expectations for how things will turn out. When you enter into experiences expectation-free, you will avoid the low end of your crash-out wave.

The Strengths of a Defined Solar Plexus
- Have consistent access to your feelings
- Rely on your defined channels as a focus for your feelings
- Can ride the wave of your emotions before making decisions
- Develop clarity over time

The Challenges of a Defined Solar Plexus
- Struggle to accept there is never 100 percent certainty in decision-making
- Must learn how to navigate and grapple with the emotional waves you experience
- Struggle with living in a world where you are expected to be happy all the time
- Feel pressure to make decisions before you are ready

Action Tips for a Defined Solar Plexus
- Accept that you will never have 100 percent buy-in with your decisions—80 percent is a yes/no.
- Pause and create space before responding.
- Learn to be an observer of your emotions vs. a bystander.
- Take ownership of your emotions especially when it comes to others.
- Use creativity as an outlet to express your emotions—emotions are simple feelings that want to be heard.

The Undefined Solar Plexus: 47 Percent of the Population

With an undefined solar plexus, you will be open emotionally; however, to the outside world (and perhaps to yourself), you might not relate to this. Many with an undefined solar plexus oscillate between being overwhelmed by feelings and not having any feelings at all. This is in part due to the fact that the undefined solar plexus takes in the feelings of those around them and then amplifies them. They are a filter sucking in the emotions that they are surrounded by.

Those with an undefined solar plexus may often experience big bursts or outbursts of emotions. They may "seem" emotionally unstable to others when in fact they are simply mirroring and amplifying the emotions of the environment they are in. Due to this, this center is especially subject to conditioning.

When the solar plexus is undefined, these people have a keen awareness of the feelings of others. They can sense it and are deeply empathetic. The challenge of having an undefined solar plexus is discerning what is yours and what is not via the gates you have and then learning to create awareness around what is actually yours and what is not.

With this center undefined, you will still have access to all of the many emotions of this center. It is important to learn that you are not your emotions (this is true for defined solar plexus as well). It is simply something you are experiencing. Learning to observe emotions and not identify with them is a challenge.

The Strengths of an Undefined Solar Plexus
- Have the gift of being on an even keel and unemotional
- Tend to be incredibly empathetic and have the ability to deeply feel what others are experiencing
- Tend to be an objective observer of the health of the emotional environment around you

The Challenges of an Undefined Solar Plexus
- Have the gift of being on an even keel and unemotional
- Struggle to be transparent/truthful so you don't hurt other people's feelings
- May feel like something is wrong with you because you are "unemotional"
- Struggle to let go of emotions and emotional patterns that never belonged to you—i.e., emotional waves

Action Tips for an Undefined Solar Plexus
- Create awareness and understanding around which "feelings" and emotions are actually yours by the gates coming off of your solar plexus.
- Establish a practice where you regularly clean the filter of your solar plexus.
- Establish practices that help you get into your body to remain grounded and not get swept away by the emotional wave of others—i.e., somatic and bodywork exercises, meditation.

- Learn to be an observer of others' emotions vs. a bystander.
- Enjoy alone time every day to dispel the emotions of others.
- Learn to step out of the room when it becomes emotionally charged.

The Not-Self of the Solar Plexus

When the solar plexus is undefined, it is subject to conditioning, and this is often a place where those who struggle do due to the fact that their emotions are a mirror. It can be deeply conditioned from a very early age. Learning to discern when you are in the not-self of the solar plexus is important. Remember, the not-self of the mind is the spokesperson for all of the undefined centers, telling us what to say and do.

The not-self of the undefined solar plexus sounds like…

- I don't want to go there because then I will have to deal with x.
- Let's go here instead of there.
- Let's not say this or that because that will upset this person.
- It is easier for me to just say nothing than to say my truth.
- I don't want to upset this person, so I will just be quiet.
- Let's just smile and agree so we don't rock the boat.
- I'm afraid if I tell the truth, I will hurt their feelings.
- I might be rejected.
- It's not worth it.
- There is no point in going there/dealing with this.
- I am so emotional; what's wrong with me?
- I don't feel any emotions; what is wrong with me?

The Gates of the Solar Plexus

- Gate 6—The Big Family/Multibusiness Entrepreneur: I support you in spotting what needs to be corrected in order for you to live in congruence with your highest, most joyous expression. I answer the question "What needs to be reckoned with/tended to/healed/fixed/corrected/improved upon in order to fulfill its potential?"
- Gate 37—The Community Maestro: I support you with my awareness of who is going to provide what is needed for you to be successful. I answer

the questions "Who do I need next to better support me? Who can provide what is needed?"

- Gate 22—The Grace Giver: I support you in tapping into your passions, desires, and creativity. I answer the question "What passion do I deeply desire to pursue that will transform the world?"

- Gate 36—The Compassionate Depth Giver: I support you with my ability to handle emotional ups and downs by moving from pain to pleasure, inexperience to experience. I answer the question "Could you share your experience of _____ with me?"

- Gate 49—The Revolution Leader: I support you with my ability to uphold my principles and see the value in myself. I answer the questions "Who and what is needed in order to make _____ happen? Is this person no longer valuing me? What do I need to let go of in order to make space for transformation/revolution in order to live in congruence with a higher set of principles so that I can expand?"

- Gate 55—The Spirited Artist: I support people with finding the right state in order to create. I answer the question "What practice do I need to cultivate to get into a creative flow? What can I do to deepen my trust so that I will be able to tap into my creativity?"

- Gate 30—The Intense Predictor: I support others by following my own dreams and bringing them to fruition while balancing my intensity. I answer the question "What am I yearning for, what am I passionate about, or what do I desire?"

The Solar Plexus Center in Biz & the Real World

The solar plexus center is the third awareness center in the body, and it was the last to evolve. It is also a motor. In the body, this is associated with the kidneys, pancreas, prostate gland, and nervous system. The seven gates of the solar plexus are patterns of fear that often are experienced as nervousness in the body that we must learn to contend with.

This is the only awareness center that is also a motor, so when this nervousness erupts in our bodies, it can spread throughout the body. It comes in waves that ebb and flow in peaks and valleys that can sweep you away. While these fears may seem valid in the moment, truth and clarity emerge with the passing of time.

The Fears of the Solar Plexus
- Gate 36—Inadequacy/Crisis
- Gate 22—Silence/Lack of Growth/Not Heard
- Gate 37—Tradition/Belonging/Broken Promises
- Gate 6—Intimacy/Vulnerability/Open
- Gate 49—Nature/Rejection/Integrity
- Gate 55—Emptiness/Passion/Moodiness
- Gate 30—Fate/Feeling/Future

The solar plexus is where we get swept away by our emotions. This is where we humans make mountains out of molehills. We get caught up in all the things. It takes us out of alignment often because we make decisions from an emotional high or an emotional low.

The emotional solar plexus colors and influences so much of the world. Since the undefined solar plexus amplifies (often two times as much) as the defined solar plexus, this can be a great source of fear, anxiety, nervousness, and disruption in the world. Since more than 50 percent of the population is defined emotionally, this center flavors the world around us, as it is both an awareness center and a motor. It's ever present in our world today. This center houses our guilt, fears, feelings, emotions, and sensitivities. It operates in waves and patterns.

The goal for either definition with this center is to learn compassion for yourself and the emotions that you experience along the way. The more you can learn to find compassion for yourself, the easier it will be to contend with the waves of the solar plexus.

The solar plexus operates in cycles. From hope to pain, from expectation to disappointment, from joy to despair, and back again. As we learn to cope with our emotional wave, instead of repeating cycles, we can begin to spiral up from the lessons learned in this center as we become more in congruence with ourselves. The goal for all of us is to learn to recognize the "flag on the field" of our lives that is the emotional wave, recognize the pattern/cycle of it, accept it, and move on from it by rising above.

This emotional motor can operate quickly, which is why it often sweeps us away. For us as a species to achieve emotional stability, we have to first understand this emotional motor and then recognize and transcend it. Therefore, it is imperative we all begin to understand how this center operates because it is the cause of a lot of collective chaos in our world today. When we can each find inner peace, we can then begin to see things as they are instead of from the heightened sense of our emotional lows or our emotional highs.

Since this is an awareness center and a motor, the way this energy is experienced is related to fears in the body, and these fears within the solar plexus emerge as nervousness. The fears in this center are not static like those of the spleen and the ajna. They move through us like waves. They come and they go. It is only once we have emerged on the other side can we truly know what is correct for those with the defined solar plexus.

SPLENIC CENTER

There is vibrance in living a life free of fear—alert to all that surrounds us, the joy of being alive, and the well-being that comes with being in the present.

Affirmation: I am not my fears. They are the tools that keep me alert to threats in my environment. It is through this alertness that I truly live. I am alive. I am adaptable. I thrive. I find joy in the moment. I trust my intuition. I rely on my senses to provide me with guidance. It is a source of inner wisdom that whispers from within.

The Source of Survival

Splenic Center—Awareness Center—Intuition, instincts, fears, body awareness, immune system time.

The splenic center is one of three awareness centers. It's concerned with our survival and vitality. This is the oldest center in the body—its most common function is to keep us alive, literally. This is our primal instinct to survive despite the odds.

This center operates in the now; it is alert and instinctual, and it drives the fear of what threatens our livelihood. Before modern society, this is the center that kept us alive—the inner alerts that guided us not to eat the red berries or to be on the lookout for animals that might attack us. This is the body's intelligence of what we need to survive, adapt, and thrive. The spleen takes in information from the environment via the five senses—sight, sound, smell, taste, and touch—then discerns whether it is in balance or whether there is something to alert us of. It has an existential awareness to it and processes this information in the now.

Every gate coming off the spleen is tied to a primary fear as it relates to survival. The splenic center's alertness builds confidence over time as we confront and survive fear-filled challenges that threaten our survival and well-being. Learning to dance with the fears that are present within our chart, be in the present and see the fear for what it is, acknowledge it, and then move on is key. The seven fears that are present in the spleen are

1. Inadequacy
2. Future
3. Past
4. Responsibility
5. Failure
6. Death/lack of purpose/meaning
7. Authority

The splenic center is where our body consciousness comes from, our spontaneity, our health, our taste, and our well-being (the splenic center is where the immune system resides) and where our values emerge from. The spleen is also responsible for the sense of time, our lightheartedness, laughter, spontaneity, and daring.

The Defined Spleen: 55 Percent of the Population

The defined spleen operates in the here and now. It is that gut feeling, hunch, or intuition.

Those with a defined spleen can often take their health for granted. It is important to allow for a complete recovery before returning to activity.

The spleen has this air of confidence and lightness to it when healthy. It has a healthy glow, a vitality of alertness, and a joy for this present moment. The healthy spleen is free of fear, filled with joy, and has a deep knowing that it can handle any survival situation that it is presented with. The spleen meets each moment with a freshness, well-being, and ease. The defined spleen has a yearning to be spontaneous.

Fear sends us out of our bodies. In order to connect with this center, we need to learn to wake up fears and dance with them. We must move our mindset from fear to alertness. With a healthy connection to the spleen, we have a natural alertness instead of a fear. A relaxed sense of alertness is more effective than fear. Meeting our fears and seeing them for what they are is a key part of grappling with this center and creating connection. With a defined spleen, you broadcast your fears out into the world. Create compassion for your fears. You are not your fears. The more we identify with our fears, the more they take over and we cut off access to our defined spleen.

Learning to build a relationship with the defined spleen is incredibly important, although as an awareness center, it is the weakest of the three. This speaks to the fragility of our lives. The more you build a connection with this center, the more confidence you will build, and the more you will step away from the fear of the gates and into the well-being and vitality of this center. Leaning into your strategy and authority while connecting with your spleen will help you achieve well-being. If not, burnout is inevitable. The way in which you access you intuition will be determined by the gates and channels you have coming off of your spleen.

The Strengths of a Defined Spleen
- Can consistently tap into your intuition
- Can use your five senses—touch, taste, smell, sight, and sound—to keep you alert and aware in the now
- Have a strong immune system and a grounded sense of vitality in the present, when healthy

The Challenges of a Defined Spleen
- Can struggle with the not-self of the mind overriding the gut instinct of the spleen
- Struggle with not being grounded and in the body—especially in the world we live in today

- Can have access to your intuition cut off
- Take your health for granted by pushing past your limits and not caring for your body

Action Tips for a Defined Spleen

- Create regular practices to help you stay in your body—figure out what works for you and stay connected to it on a regular basis.
- Be in the present—moment to moment.
- Shift your mindset from fear to alertness.
- Use meditation to root and ground you in the present.
- Journal on your fears.

The Undefined Spleen: 45 Percent of the Population

The seven primal fears all reside in the spleen, and when the center is undefined, those fears can be amplified. For the undefined spleen, it is important to face each of those fears one by one in order to become "fearless"—it is in this facing of the fears that one learns awareness around each of the fears.

Those with an undefined spleen can sense the lack of well-being in the world and the fears of others. They will often carry these fears, especially from childhood, and internalize them. They may find a sense of safety from those with a defined spleen and create an attachment (which can often lead to an unhealthy codependence).

It is important for those with an undefined spleen to establish a healthy relationship with this center. Discerning what is yours and letting go of the conditioning of this center are critical. This is a highly sensitive center since it is concerned with survival and our primary fears. Relying on your strategy and authority with an undefined spleen rather than the conditioning of others is important.

The undefined spleen is a gift when you peel back the conditioning that you have taken on in the world. It is highly intuitive, although it cannot be relied on for decision-making. The undefined spleen has a keen sense of what is healthy for others and can provide you with a wealth of knowledge.

The Strengths of an Undefined Spleen
- Learn to discern which fears and anxieties are yours
- Have a keen sense of what is healthy for others
- Offer deep wisdom for others—a healer of sorts
- Can be incredibly intuitive
- Have a groundedness in clarity
- Have a nonreactive alertness
- Can witness fear without identifying with it
- Tend to be more sensitive of your body

The Challenges of an Undefined Spleen
- Tend to lose track of time or feel pressured by time
- Prone to taking in and amplifying everyone's fears and anxieties
- Can feel like the world doesn't have your back
- Attracted to people with a defined spleen in order to feel safe
- Tend to hold on to things longer than what feels right—relationships, jobs, etc.
- May be sensitive to illness or have a sensitive immune system
- Identify with other's sicknesses
- Don't enjoy being spontaneous

Action Tips for an Undefined Spleen
- Clear the filter of your undefined spleen—energy medicine and meditation can be helpful.
- Be in the present—moment to moment.
- Become an observer of fears without taking them on or identifying with them.
- Embrace that you are open to the world and don't have to live fearfully.
- Appreciate the many superpowers that come with an undefined spleen.

The Not-Self of the Undefined Spleen
The mind is the not-self spokesperson for all of the centers in the body. It is no different with the spleen. The not-self of the undefined spleen can sound like . . .

- I'm just going to hold on for another day.
- It will get better tomorrow.
- I'm insecure because . . .
- Let's not do that because I'm afraid of . . .
- I'm not going to say that because it will upset _____.
- I'm afraid of *insert fear*.
- This person might leave if I . . .
- I might fail.
- I'm not good enough.
- I'm going to settle for this relationship because I'm afraid I won't find another.
- I'm overwhelmed with anxiety because I feel scared of this action (or what this person might think or say).

The Gates of the Spleen

- Gate 18—The Critic: I support you in spotting what needs to be corrected in order for you to live in congruence with your highest, most joyous expression. I answer the question "What needs to be reckoned with/tended to/healed/fixed/corrected/improved upon in order to fulfill its potential?"
- Gate 48—The Well of Wisdom: I support you in seeing a new solution based on the depth of knowledge I have. I answer the question "What does it look like to come up with something new?"
- Gate 57—The Insightful Intuitive: I support you with my intuitive hits and my instinctive knowing. I answer the question "Do you have a knowing or instinct for me?"
- Gate 44—The Talent Scout: I support you with my ability to spot talent and heal past patterns of mistakes. I answer the questions "Who has the skill to be in this role? What patterns need to be healed in order for me to break through my limiting beliefs?"
- Gate 50—The Caring Parent: I support you with challenging your values and elevating your well-being. I answer the question "What values might I need to reconsider in order to better nurture, nourish, and elevate myself?"
- Gate 32—The Successful Conservative: I support you with my ability to see the value of things and discern what next step/investment will

support long-term success. I answer the question "What foundation do I need to have in place in order to achieve _____?"

- Gate 28—The Risk Taker: I support you in discerning what is worth fighting for/taking a risk for in life. I answer the questions "What is my purpose in life? What risk is worth taking?"

The Splenic Center in Biz & the Real World

The splenic center speaks in the now. It is our intuition, gut response, and knowing in the now. It is our ability to discern what is safe for us in the now. It is the ability to spontaneously judge what is correct or not for us. It is here to keep us alive, and it is concerned with our survival. All awareness centers are rooted in fear. Each of the centers has its own frequency with how fear shows up, and the spleen is no different. The spleen houses the seven primal fears that happen in the now and are related to survival itself.

1. Gate 48—Inadequacy
2. Gate 57—Future
3. Gate 44—Past
4. Gate 50—Responsibility
5. Gate 32—Failure
6. Gate 28—Death/lack of purpose/meaning
7. Gate 18—Authority

In business, this center often emerges as the gut response or inner knowing, which from my experience with entrepreneurs, is often ignored because it doesn't always make sense or isn't the typical way things are done in the industry. The splenic center, regardless of definition, gives each of us an instinct or a hunch about what is correct for us or not. This is felt as the inner nudge to do something even when it might not make sense.

In my own experience, I felt this when I began to study Human Design. It was an innate inner knowing or nudge to pursue this knowledge even though I had no idea how I would use it at the time.

Many entrepreneurs ignore or dismiss these gut feelings only to later think, *I wish I had followed that gut instinct.* That is how this center works; it is instinctual and in the moment. It is not designed to make sense. It is simply designed to keep you alive and support you in vitality.

Conversely, this center, because it is associated with the seven primal fears, can also keep entrepreneurs stuck in indecision. I have seen this emerge as

- Waffling back and forth and never moving forward out of fear of what might happen
- Providing lots of criticism from the sidelines on others but never actually taking action for oneself
- Feeling like you don't know enough or have enough knowledge so you take one more course even though you could teach the class
- Getting swept away fighting for things that don't matter
- Being so afraid to invest in resources that you never move forward
- Caring for everyone but yourself

Obviously, as an entrepreneur, any of these things would be challenging to contend with, particularly if you want to grow your business. The key with this center, regardless of definition, is to create a healthy relationship with the fears you experience. We must learn to have an alertness with respect to our fears, and it is through the splenic center that we find that alertness. We dance with it, we honor it, but we do not let it stop us from moving forward.

With people who have an undefined spleen, I am always mindful that these are people who may hold onto things longer than they ought to. When working with an undefined spleen, there is often a rationalization for why the person is tolerating x. For example, many of those with an undefined spleen will continue working with a client or in a business container even though they are certain it is not for them. This is because they fear what will happen if they don't have that.

I always like to ask and consider when working with the undefined spleen, what foundation do I need to have in place in order to move forward? This can be supportive to both the undefined spleen and the defined spleen counterparts who are in the low expression of this center.

SACRAL CENTER

There is truth in the now—the moment to moment. There is a fire that bubbles up from within, pulling, pushing, responding, providing guidance . . . now.

Affirmation: When I embody my strategy and author-ity, I will always have the energy to bring my dreams to life. I honor the calls, the response, the invitation, or the initiation, and I take action knowing that with the right calls, the power is behind me. I honor my body's cues for rest. I know with great specificity that I am at my best when I prioritize myself. I fill my own cup first, and self-care happens first. I am full of vitality, energy, and momentum.

The Source of Energy & Action

Sacral Center—Vital energy, fertility, availability, response.

Let's talk about the sacral center: the source of all energy and action. This center is a powerful and complex motor center. All life on the planet is fostered by the creative life force energy that originates within this center.

The sacral center fuels us to take action, work, move, respond, reproduce, propel forward, and persist. The sacral is designed to provide answers in the moment to moment. Regardless of being defined or undefined, this center can be a source of major burnout, especially when not cared for.

The sacral is a source of drive and momentum that we feel to move forward. This is the most powerful motor in the whole chart. It is literally what keeps our species going forward since this is where creation happens. The sacral sets the standard for the energetic force and impact that the human race operates within.

The Defined Sacral: 70 Percent of the Population

Nearly 70 percent of the population has a defined sacral (it will be colored in red if it is defined—the second square up from the bottom of the chart). When the sacral is defined, you have a built-in guidance system to provide you with yes (uh-huh) or no (ut-huh) answers in the moment.

Your job with a defined sacral is to find work you love and become the master of that work. You fall asleep at the end of the day exhausted, satisfied, and fulfilled from a day's work. The next day, you wake up renewed with a sense of exuberance and vitality to do it all over again.

Learning to trust and access this inner knowing is key, and many adults have been disconnected from their sacral response. Have a person you trust ask you a yes/no question to help you tap back into that energy. The response should come from within your gut, and it may take time to reconnect with it. It will almost feel like a bodily pull or push. Generator children will provide you with an example of this. Ask them yes/no questions and witness the sacral energy's power.

The defined sacral energy is here to work in response. You have consistent access to energy. That energy is intended to be used up each and every single day doing work you love. The challenge is only saying yes to and doing the work you love, otherwise burnout and frustration are inevitable.

There is enormous potential in this center in our world today if we can get more people responding, knowing themselves, and doing work they love. When you have the full power of a response behind a decision, the follow-through power of the sacral is incredible.

The Defined Sacral Connection

The Sacral to the Throat—With this configuration of the sacral connected directly or indirectly to the throat, this is the generative force that is ready to manifest. This configuration often presents itself as a physical response (pull or push) in the body. For example, in real life, if you were to ask someone with this configuration, "Would you like to do x?" these people would immediately stand up and take action. This can show up as words, but it is a flag of caution. They may need to then respond to that response and give themselves the space to change their mind.

The Sacral to the Spleen—With this configuration, the sacral response emerges as sounds that are discerning what is healthy or not. This is a response to what is happening in life through the immune system. This is the sacral response of vitality and being alive.

The Sacral to the Identity Centers—With this configuration, the sacral response emerges as the empowerment of the person's identity. This shows up as someone who relates to their sacral response—the response is moving through them as part of who they are. This may look like a surrendering to a force greater than who we are.

The Strengths of a Defined Sacral

- Have consistent access to energy—meant to be used up daily
- Have the energy to sustain your work once you are doing work you love
- Energy resets to zero every day
- The work you love will be hidden in the gates/channels coming off of the sacral
- Dance with the universe via responding
- Have a deep inner knowing

The Challenges of a Defined Sacral

- Must learn to follow your yeses and what lights you up
- Subject to burnout when you have agreed to something that isn't a full body yes
- Experience frustration when you've agreed to something that wasn't a yes
- Experience frustration when you hit a plateau

- Experience frustration when you fail to respond
- Struggle with indecision even though you know the decision
- Feel disconnected from the inner knowing the sacral provides
- Struggle with gates and channels activated in the chart

Action Tips for a Sacral

- Learn to embrace the pause, and learn to integrate and synthesize before taking action—follow your strategy and authority.
- Be vigilant in your responses.
- Leverage the power of yes/no questions.
- Get into the present moment.
- Learn to trust your sacral sounds and actually make decisions.

The Undefined Sacral: 30 Percent of the Population

The 30 percent of the population with an undefined sacral (colored in white) are not here to work in the traditional sense of the word. Undefined sacrals do not have consistent access to the life force energy of this motor center. Your energy waxes and wanes. It's here and then it's not.

The challenge with an undefined sacral is you take in and amplify the energy of others—both the thriving powerful energy of the defined sacral and the burned-out fatigued energy. This results in not knowing when or how to shut off. It is almost like a light switch that is broken and stuck in the on position. Undefined sacrals often don't know when enough is enough.

With an undefined sacral, you might find yourself working longer and harder than those around you. That is because you are amplifying the energy of 70 percent of the population. You are not meant to work this way, and you will burn out if you stay on this path. You are not an energy being.

Creating healthy boundaries and understanding how you connect with others via your strategy and authority are key to those of us with an undefined sacral. Understanding that you have a deep need for rest and honoring the ebbs and flows of your energy while observing the powerful responding energy generated by 70 percent of the population is critical.

With an undefined sacral, it is your job to become strategic with how you use your energy. As you begin to realize that you are different from most in our society, you will begin to see the gifts in your strategic energy. An undefined sacral gives you a special gift that most don't have, and it is an essential part of humanity.

The Strengths of an Undefined Sacral
- Have the ability to pause and live with ease and balance
- Have the gift of being able to relax
- Not designed to work in the traditional sense of the word or in a sustainable ongoing way
- Can enrich the lives of others with the wisdom you provide—Manifestors with initiating, Projectors with guiding, and Reflectors with reflecting
- Have the ability to magnetize people to you when in your strategy and authority
- Accept that you are different from 70 percent of the population

The Challenges of an Undefined Sacral
- Susceptible to burnout
- Feel like you aren't doing enough
- Subject to being easily overwhelmed
- Struggle to know when enough is enough
- Tend to burn the candle at both ends
- Face challenges with the gates you have activated
- Struggle to find the right timing
- Feel a great deal of pressure to do and be in the doing
- Need more "rest" than most
- Struggle to do nothing

Action Tips for an Undefined Sacral
- Get into bed before you are tired so that you don't miss your body's cues to fall asleep.
- Prioritize rest.

- Clear out your sacral of what doesn't belong to you—to do this, spend time in nature, spend alone time, or give yourself space.
- Prioritize your self-care above all else. You cannot share your gifts if you don't have the energy to do so.
- Be grounded in the present moment.

The Not-Self of the Sacral

When the sacral center is undefined, it is subject to conditioning. The mind is the not-self spokesperson for all undefined centers. The not-self of the undefined sacral sounds like . . .

- I'll just do this one more thing.
- We've got to keep working.
- FOMO aka fear of missing out
- We need to get this done.
- We are going to miss out if we don't say yes.
- I can keep going.
- Yes, we can do that too.
- I'm not tired yet.
- I don't want to take a nap, there is too much to do.
- Who better than me to get the work done? Someone has got to do it.
- What are boundaries?
- I must be doing something. I can't sit still.

The Gates of the Sacral

- Gate 5—The Consistent Dependable: I support you by showing up in a dependable, consistent, and habitual manner. I can be relied on to be routine, consistent. I answer the question "What can we systematize, productize, or make routine?"
- Gate 14—The Resourceful Creative: I support you in discerning which skills (and the commitment) are needed to bring a new creative project to life in the world. I answer the questions "What creative project is correct for me based on who I am? What skills/time commitment do I need to bring this to life?"

- Gate 29—The Tenacious Persistent: I support you with my determination and persistence because I show you what is possible in the world. I answer the questions "Is this really possible? Am I really committed to doing _____?"

- Gate 59—The Intimate Creative: I support you with my ability to create and sustain people and business endeavors. I answer the questions "Is this sustainable and does it support the foundation I am building in life/biz? Who can I collaborate with?"

- Gate 9—The Immersed: I support you in seeing what is of value to focus on (or not). I answer the question "What is worthy/deserving of my time/energy/effort to focus on?"

- Gate 3—The Innovator: I support you with my tenacity, structure, patience, and inventiveness. I answer the questions "How can I be more disciplined so that I can find the limitations of this structure to innovate? What will have a lasting impact in the world?"

- Gate 42—The Finisher: I support you with my ability to finish. I answer the questions "What can you help me finish? What needs to be completed so that I can start something new?"

- Gate 27—The Protective Caregiver: I support you with how I nourish and prioritize myself first and set the example for self-care. I answer the questions "What can I do to better nourish myself so that I can thrive? How can I hold myself accountable to take better care of myself?"

- Gate 34—The Empowered Individual: I support you when I own my own power and use it wisely. I answer the question "Where do I need to allow pull instead of push in my life?"

The Sacral Center in Biz & the Real World

The Defined Sacral

One of the features of the sacral center that is important to consider is that it has its own frequency. With nine gates, it is the second most complex center in the chart after the throat. This center gives off a frequency and can speak through the sacral response via sounds or through physical action. It "speaks" as a burst of energy but can only ever emerge in response to others. This sacral response often emerges as sacral sounds of uh-huh and ut-huh, but it can also emerge as language if it is directly connected to the throat, as a physical body response with a surge in energy.

The sacral vibrates out the sacral sounds through the diaphragm in the body. While the sacral and the throat are similar, the throat is the hub for all of the centers in the body, while the sacral is *the* most powerful motor in the body. If you think about the throat, it can initiate conversation, while the sacral response is a noise or a grunt. True communication in our day and age does not start with an uh-huh or ut-huh. It starts with words. This dichotomy sums up why the sacral center must be in response instead of initiating. Yet, so many of our sacral beings are taught from a very young age to initiate; however, this is not correct for them.

The sacral is responsible for life force energy. This energy operates in a vortex—spiraling the body. Once a Generator or an MG has had a sacral "yes" response, the light switch of their energy is turned on. This vortex remains on from birth until death; however, the sacral needs periods of rest to refuel. If the Generator or MG has bypassed their sacral response, then the sacral will start to de-energize, meaning burnout and exhaustion may result.

As with all centers in Human Design, the sacral at its high expression is either creative and energizing or at its low expression de-energizing and destructive. With a defined sacral, you will have a constant energy buzz; it is simply about understanding how that energy is directed in order to discern how it will be expressed—high expression or low expression.

The frequency of the sacral energy must go somewhere and do something. If it is not expressed, it can turn into mindlessly doing tasks just to burn off the energy that is present, usually expressed through repeated activities—fiddling with something, incessant cleaning, or organizing the same thing over and over again. This is the energy of not being able to sit still. Sacral energy must be used up each and every day since it resets to zero.

Frustration, Sticktuitiveness, and the Sacral Center—If you have a defined sacral center, frustration is a part of your experience. Frustration for sacral beings is not a bad thing; think of frustration as a compass. If you are sacrally defined, for every activity you enter into there will be a plateau or a barrier of frustration that you will bump up against.

If you can persist with that activity in spite of frustration, then that is the correct thing for you. If you cannot, then it is likely that it is time to move on. That frustration is a sign that it is either time to dig deeper or let go. It is in this digging deeper that transformation happens. This is the sticktuitiveness to stay with the process in order to transform into something better.

For sacral beings, if the activity is correct, they can endure and become very expert, but they have to love what they are doing. The length of this "stuckness" in to order to improve varies. Then one day, they simply just improve, and while they don't often realize it at the time, it happens. If you are sacrally defined, you are here to master and commit to something—your job is to discern what you are here to become a master at. This is the gift of a sacral being—owning an expertise.

The challenge with this is that the not-self of the mind often takes over and labels the sacral being as a quitter because they can't seem to stick with anything. Yet, this is their process. Learning to contend with this not-self talk of the mind is critical in order to find the thing you are here to master as a sacral being. These periods of being stuck and feeling frustrated are a natural part of their life.

In business, I see so many Generators and MGs behaving like Manifestors by initiating themselves into things without honoring that sacral response. They often end up in great frustration because they are starting things instead of responding. The challenge here lies in tapping back into their sacral response. The sounds of the sacral were how our ancestors communicated before the development of language in the throat—through the grunts, sounds, and noises that emerged in this center. The true sacral response only comes in the form of a response. If it is in response, the actions taken next will be correct for the sacral being. They will then be able to generate the energy in order to follow through or hit a point of frustration either diving deeper or moving on to the next thing. It is in their responding they can discern what is correct for them or their truth as well as the level of their energy.

Generators and MGs are often taught from a very young age to "use their words" and are often initiating from early on as well. This results in them having little to no connection with their sacral response when in reality this is their power and truth. Once a sacral being initiates, they lose all of their power. Learning to honor (and trust) the sacral sounds that emerge becomes the key component for these people, coupled with letting go of the things they don't want to stick to.

In the nonentrepreneurial world, it is often important to consider that 70 percent of the population is defined sacrally. When you think about the frustration around work and the corporate nine-to-five, so many sacral beings are trapped in a place of frustration not doing work that they love, and ultimately, they burn out their sacral.

The response of the sacral does not take into consideration the awareness centers that may be present in the body. When in a relationship, this means someone who is a defined throat person may want an explanation to the response of the sacral centers. The throat person needs a reason or a why behind the "no" of the sacral person. But the sacral response doesn't have an explanation as it doesn't tap into the awareness centers to make a decision. This is where sacral beings begin to lose their power and connection with their sacral response because they are forced to come up with a why, but that why is for the other and often leads to the not-self taking over and making decisions from the mind instead of the sacral response.

As a result of this needing to explain, the sacral beings are often convinced by others to "do work" that is not in response to their sacral. Many of the world's biggest frustrations are built on the backs of sacral beings who have been convinced by the other types to do work that is not a sacral yes for them. The sacral beings *must* learn to trust their response and not allow the need to explain themselves to others take over. Therefore, learning to wait and be patient to have something to respond to is critical for the elimination or at least reduction of frustration for the sacral beings.

The defined sacral operates in a cycle of waiting to respond, responding, getting stuck/frustrated, moving to another level or moving on, and then getting stuck again. Repeating over and over again.

The Undefined Sacral

For those with an undefined sacral, you are under a near constant state of conditioning from the 70 percent of the population who is defined sacrally. Those who have an undefined sacral at its high expression simply want to relax and allow others to do the work . . . *or not*. The undefined sacral is often incredibly conditioned and stuck in the on position.

Undefined sacral beings are sensitive to both the people and places that they surround themselves with. In business, this often appears as them doing more than their defined peers because they are taking in the energy of those who are defined and mirroring it back to them. This sacral energy being amplified in the non-sacral being's body is unideal. The undefined sacral beings cannot sustain "doing" like their defined counterparts.

The non-sacral beings often present themselves as the busiest person in the room stuck in the on position. Yet, that energy is not their own; it is simply the amplification of those they are surrounded by. They borrow the energy of the sacral beings in their life, which is why people and place become vital to the health of the undefined sacral. If they are around a sacral being who is at a low expression, the non-sacral being amplifies that. Conversely, the opposite is also true.

Non-sacrally defined beings' bodies are not equipped to handle the life force energy flowing through their aura and subsequently their bodies. The systems of non-sacral beings are very sensitive, and if they are not discerning about who they are around and what place they are in, they end up conditioned.

A great metaphor for a non-sacral being to remember is to pretend you own a diesel car, but you end up putting regular gasoline in it instead. That is not the correct fuel for your car to operate with, and it will likely cause issues over time. The same goes for defined sacral beings in a non-sacral being's life. The non-sacral being can end up burned out, exhausted, and overworked when they have the wrong aura (and place) in their life. This is why it is key for non-sacral beings to be sure they have the correct people in their life.

Undefined sacral centers can often feel the shift in energy or the low expression of the defined sacral beings before they even notice. This is how sensitive the undefined sacral is. It is important to remember that the sacral center is the source of our doing and our sexuality. It is the source of creation in this world. In relationships, the undefined sacral simply mirrors back what the defined sacral is experiencing. The undefined sacral is a barometer of the defined sacrals in their life.

In business, this energy often presents as wanting to do all the things and not being able to say no. It shows up in "doing" all of the things. I often think of the saying "If you want something done, ask a busy person." I believe this was written for non-sacral beings, as non-sacral beings can often get more done than their sacral counterparts due to conditioning.

In reality, the aligned and not-conditioned expression of this center shows us a new way to operate in the world that operates in ebbs and flows vs. consistency and persistence. It becomes imperative for those who are undefined to not identify with the life force energy that flows through them.

Learning to tune into the energy of what is their own and what are they amplifying is key because the buzzy frequency of the defined sacral is ever present in this world. Non-sacral beings need to allow those who are sacrally defined to leverage it instead of allowing it to take over their body and bypass their signals of when it is time to stop, which is often what happens.

This is because this world is designed for sacral beings—people who can do and take action. We live in a culture where our ability to do and achieve is often tied to our worth. Non-sacral beings have the ability to work, but they need to do work they love and delegate the rest of the work they don't want to do to others.

Burnout is very common in non-sacral beings. They overcommit, overdo, and push their body beyond the limits of what it is capable of. They struggle to create solid boundaries for themselves, and therefore, struggle to say no to things even when they know it is beyond their capabilities. Non-sacral beings are put under tremendous pressure to work and produce. This results in exhaustion and a feeling of overwhelm because of other people's energy.

When a non-sacral being steps out of the aura of their sacral counterparts, they often realize they cannot sustain the workload they committed to, and they lose confidence and crash. Their body betrays them because they overworked it. Many non-sacral beings will face bouts of burnout until they can learn to cleanse themselves of the borrowed doing energy of their sacral counterparts. The non-sacral must learn to know when to withdraw and recharge by setting clear boundaries and listening to their body when it comes to what they can accomplish.

ROOT CENTER

There is ever present pressure to do in this fast-paced world. More, more, more is never enough, and it drives the stress we feel.

Affirmation: I am not my stress. I am calm, grounded, and rooted in the present. I honor the pressure I feel to do, and I align with my strategy and authority before stepping into action. The pressure to do when fueled by authority gives me the strength to follow through in a way that is congruent with my unique being. I honor the ever present pressure and allow my strategy and authority to drive me. I am enough. I am whole. I am rooted here in the moment.

The Root of All Stress

Root Center—Motor & Pressure Center—Physical pressure, life, fuel, adrenaline, drive, stress, worry.

The root center is one of two pressure centers, and it is the square at the bottom of the Human Design chart. It is the pressure and stress "to do." It is literally the source of all stress in the body. The pressure inside of the root is what gets the body into momentum and action in life. What we do with that stress energy will determine whether the stress we experience is good or bad for the body.

The root center is both a motor center and a pressure center (like the head). This center literally gets and keeps the body in momentum or in action. The motor of the root operates as pulsing. On . . . off . . . on . . . off. This means you may have periods of time where you experience more pressure since the root is off and the pressure of this center is building.

Since the root is one of two pressure centers in the body, it will always have a connection to the head (the pressure to know). There is a certain duality between these two centers that fuels the human species forward. If you have a defined head and root, it will be important for you to create practices to relieve pressure.

This charged energy (almost like a bottled lightning bolt) brings the pressure and the fuel to evolve and adapt to the world and its many challenges. It is a powerful force, and one that is important to learn how to manage and grapple with. Since the root is the source of stress in the body, it can wreak havoc on the physical body when not managed properly.

For you, which gates or channels are activated will determine which pressures you experience and how you experience them. The gates or channels that are connected or reaching for the sacral drive the fuel to action. The gates or channels reaching for the solar plexus are concerned with feelings and emotional responses. The gates or channels reaching for the spleen are the drive to survive and thrive.

The Defined Root: 60 Percent of the Population

With a defined root, you will have a fixed way you handle stress and pressure in the world based on your unique configuration within your Human Design chart. Learning to get to know this pressurized energy is key in order to live in congruence with your design. You can learn to wield the power of this pressure, focus it, and use it to make an impact in service of others.

The Strengths of a Defined Root
- Have consistent access to your drive and an innate ability to be in action
- Can handle pressure, the buildup of pressure, and use it wisely
- Able to focus your drive and channel this energy that inspires others to act

The Challenges of a Defined Root

- Must understand that timing is critical when working with pulsing energy of the root
- Can feel out of whack with your strategy and authority due to the initiating energy of the defined root
- Experience burnout when you are out of congruence with your strategy and authority

Action Tips for a Defined Root

- Create a regular exercise practice that helps you relieve pressure from the root—think something that makes you sweat (as always though consult with your physician to determine whether this type of exercise is right for you).
- When in doubt, fall back on your strategy and authority.
- There may be times when you feel pressure but struggle to get into action. Be patient for the pulse of the root to turn back on again.

The Undefined Root: 40 Percent of the Population

With an undefined root, you are constantly taking in pressure from the rest of the population with a defined root and amplifying this energy. It can be difficult for those with an undefined root to be under this near constant energy of pressure. One of the most important things to realize with an undefined root is that this pressure is not yours. The pressure you feel to go and do and take on more is not yours. Learning to dispel this pressure to do from others is key.

The Strengths of an Undefined Root

- Tend to be discerning about what activities you do take action on
- Have lots of options on how you "work with stress and pressure"
- Can be very productive at times

The Challenges of an Undefined Root

- Absorb pressure and stress from your environment
- Can be very susceptible to burnout
- Struggle to get into action

Action Tips for an Undefined Root

- Create transition activities between work and home to let go of the energies that are not yours—things like doing restorative yoga, meditating, walking in nature, or dancing to a song are helpful to do "in between."
- Get to know the gates you have coming off of your root center—this will give personality to the energy that is yours.
- Learn to discern what is yours.

The Not-Self of the Root

Both defined and undefined root centers can experience the not-self themes. The not-self of the root asks

- What is my purpose in life?
- I need to figure out my passions. What am I passionate about?
- What am I going to do to make my life better?
- I have to achieve something (or more) in my life.
- _____ is ahead of me. I need to catch up. I'm behind.
- How come I can't get past this block?
- What am I doing to focus on? I need something to focus on.
- Who needs me? I must be needed.
- I feel like experiencing something new. Let me _____. (And therefore, self-sabotage.)
- Let's hurry up and find a new experience.
- Let's not waste any time.
- I must get this done.
- Just one more thing . . . I'll just do this, then I'll stop.

Learning to dance with this energy in the body is a challenge. This is a restless energy that will nag at you until you release it. It will lead you astray. Create regular practices that help you unwind like exercising, meditating, doing yoga, walking, and journaling, which are all great for both the defined and undefined roots—which you choose will depend on your definition. Find what works for you that helps you burn off the stress energy of the root.

Since both defined and undefined roots can experience the not-self (this is not true for all centers), it is important to recognize this not-self when it bubbles up from within you. The not-self of the root is best described as sort of an incessant need to do more, more, more.

The Gates of the Root

- Gate 53—The Starter: I support you with my ability to start something new—creative endeavors, projects, learnings, etc. I answer the question "What will I initiate or start?"

- Gate 60—The Change Maker: I support you with my ability to bring about lasting change in the world. I answer the question "What can I innovate, invent, or transform?"

- Gate 52—The Buddha: I support you in getting grounded in order to gain clarity. I answer the question "How can I clear my mind, still my body, and slow down in order to gain clarity on what is next?"

- Gate 19—The Thoughtful Host: I support you with my ability to shine awareness on the needs of the group or individual. I answer the questions "How can I better support my people? What aspects of support are missing?"

- Gate 39—The Provocative Artist: I support you with my ability to provoke your emotions and creativity to gain consciousness/clarity on a project. I answer the question "I am experiencing a creative block. Can you help me unleash my creativity/passions/desires?"

- Gate 41—The Possibility Dreamer: I support you with my limitless imagination and daydreams to generate new possibilities in the world. I answer the question "What new opportunity/idea do you imagine with _____?"

- Gate 58—The Delightful Spirit: I support you in spotting what needs to be corrected. I answer the question "How can we improve upon this?"

- Gate 38—The Purposeful Effortless Warrior: I support you with my ability to craft a vision and stick with it. My stubbornness and resilience ensure you do not compromise your values, purpose, or meaning in life. I answer the questions "What is my vision? Is it meaningful/original/ worth fighting for?"

- Gate 54—The Ambitious Prosperity Seeker: I support you with my ambition, influence, and drive. I answer the question "How can I achieve _____?"

The Root Center in Biz & the Real World

The root center houses some of the most powerful vital fuel in the body—the stress pressure and fuel to evolve, change, and adapt to our ever changing world. As a motor and a pressure center, this fuel is the purest form of energy in the body, yet it is too powerful to be directly connected to the throat. It must pass through either the sacral, the spleen, or the solar plexus before this energy makes its way to the throat.

The root center is concerned with the nine pressures of being alive.

1. Gate 58—to correct
2. Gate 38—to find purpose
3. Gate 54—to rise up
4. Gate 53—to begin
5. Gate 60—to mutate
6. Gate 52—to focus
7. Gate 19—to need
8. Gate 39—to find spirit
9. Gate 41—to desire

The format channels are housed in the connection between the root and the sacral. If this energy is present, it influences the rest of the Human Design chart. Channel 53-42—the beginning and ending processes of cycles. Channel 9-52—logical and concentrated processes. Channel 3-60—unpredictable and mutative processes. If a format channel or gate is present, this has an influence over the rest of your chart.

Gates 58, 38, and 54 process the pressure to stay healthy and vital in this life—connection to the spleen. While gates 19, 39, and 41 process emotional pressure—the connection to the solar plexus.

When we begin to think about stress and pressure, we must begin to think about our relationship with it. Stress isn't inherently good or inherently bad. It simply is. We are the ones who give the stress in our life meaning. Instead of befriending stress, we demonize it. We suffer from it. We allow it to run and dictate our lives. From a mechanical perspective in the body, stress is simply a fuel that energizes us. Stress allows us to handle challenging situations and become a master of them.

We live in a society that is riddled with stress, pressure, and overwhelm. This is because of our relationship with stress. We identify with it. We become overridden by it. It causes depression (particularly if format energy is present) and burnout, and it leaves us with a feeling of never being able to catch up or be enough. Part of this is our inherent need as humans to be more, do more, have more, and live in a more material way. The reality is though, we do not need to prove ourselves to others. We must learn to cope with stress based on the configuration that is present in our chart.

Our society enters into stress for the wrong reasons without much consideration for strategy and authority. In the root center, in particular, it is imperative to understand that joy and stillness are key to handling stress. It's ironic that in the center concerned with stress, understanding joy and stillness is the key. These themes of joy (gate 58) and stillness (gate 52) allow us to enter into stress properly.

When we begin something with stillness or joy, no matter what endeavor we are embarking on, we will be able to remain grounded to the root center. Gate 52 gives us the ability to remain still and inward through the stress, and gate 58 gives us the ability to rise to the challenge and meet it with joy. The secret to the root center then is to only begin things in life if they are either from a place of stillness or a sense of joy.

A Note about the Conditioning in the Root Center

When this center is undefined, it can present itself in two ways: (1) hyperactivity or (2) freezing. Many people in this world who have an undefined root center are amplifying the energy of those who have a defined root and mirroring back to those with definition their energy. The problem with this is, the undefined believe this is their energy—amplified, hyperactive, restless, and under a tremendous amount of stress and pressure.

We see this play out in classrooms where the undefined children are often scolded for their hyperactivity, yet they are simply amplifying and mirroring their defined classmates. This often results in labeling those children as "problem" children who cannot focus. These children are often accused of a lack of focus and an inability to concentrate. However, these children are in the conditioning field of their defined counterparts. It is not their inability to focus; it is the inability of their defined classmates to focus. This is a huge problem since that stress energy is not theirs. They are simply in the field of conditioning. Children in particular with an undefined root must learn to understand that the hyperactivity or not that they are experiencing is not their own. They can use this energy to have a positive impact when they are in the conditioning field, but we must educate them that they cannot identify with it.

We as a society give our authority away to the conditioning pressure of the root center, letting stress govern our lives instead of leveraging it. The pressure and stress driven from the root center can support those with an undefined root center in achieving great things, but the energy they have access to is not consistent or reliable. This energy can be channeled to thrive under pressure. For example, those with an undefined root may love to perform on stage (or not). They can use the amplification of the stress pressure to perform.

However, this undefined root energy can also present as a freeze mode—people who are completely overwhelmed by the stress pressure and freeze, unable to make decisions and move forward. These people can become completely frozen by the adrenalized energy in their body, and it can terrify them. Learning to cope with this and not identify with it becomes the key.

COMPLETELY OPEN CENTERS

There is the gift of wisdom. The depth of the ocean. The insights to light. The flame that changes the world within. Honor the gifts of the open centers.

> *Affirmation: I am free from the conditioning of others. I put down what I have been carrying that doesn't serve me. I let go of what is not mine. I embrace the unwinding, the weight, and the worry. I put down what the world thought I "should" be and am honoring what I actually am. I am me. I am free. I am fluid.*

When you have open centers in your chart, they will have no gates or channels coming off of them. This is known as completely open. This is a subset of having an undefined center with the caveat that when a center is completely open, there is no way to ground the center in knowing what is yours and what is not yours.

What this means is that there is no consistent theme to help us ground ourselves in who we are. For example, if you had an undefined throat but had gate 16, you would have a consistent theme of experimenting to ground your voice in. When the center is open, that grounding is absent.

Open centers can be feeding grounds for deep conditioning; conversely, they are also centers that have a wealth and depth of wisdom. When we can peel back the layers of what is not ours and those of others around us, society, culture, etc., we can then begin to see the beauty of these centers.

When you have an open center, there is a fluidity of your abilities and personalities within that center. Think of it as having no set or fixed way of doing something. You can choose from the array of options that lie within the gates of each center. You have no filter energy coming in through the center, and you are, therefore, open to its unlimited potential, learning, and wisdom.

The key with open centers is to discern what is yours and put down all of the "stuff" you are carrying for others. This could mean the conditioning you've picked up from someone, culture, education, family heritage, etc. I highly recommend pulling the charts of people who are present in your life (with their permission) and then seeing how they might be influencing your open centers.

Learning who you are is most important when it comes to open centers, while relying on your strategy and authority to guide you. Remember, when you have an open center or an undefined one, you will amplify the energy of the defined centers around you. For example, if you have an undefined head, you will amplify the mental pressure to know of the undefined head.

The open centers operate in extremes or polarity. When healthy, they will be a clear filter that provides a depth of wisdom for others. You, as the owner of this wisdom, will be able to observe the extremes and not attach yourself to them. You will be able to watch them as they pass through you, knowing they are not yours.

When in the not-self or unhealthy, it will often swing wildly from one extreme to the other. For example:

- Open Head—from overthinking to not thinking at all
- Open Ajna—from not knowing how to process information to overprocessing
- Open Throat—from not knowing what to say to blurting things out
- Open Heart—from having an inflated sense of worth (egocentric) to feeling worthless

- Open Identity—from not having any direction to having a set/fixed direction, from not knowing who you are to knowing who you are, or from not feeling lovable to feeling overly lovable
- Open Spleen—from being fearful of everything to not fearing anything at all
- Open Solar Plexus—from being overemotional to not being emotional at all
- Open Sacral—from excessive activity and overwhelm, typically scattered, to no activity at all
- Open Root – from excessive urgency and stress to completely frozen and stuck

Remember, open and undefined centers amplify the energy of those around. Learning to become an observer of these extremes will help you create a healthy relationship with the centers. Below you will find a bit more depth to each of the open centers.

Open Head—With an open head center, you can oscillate its thinking between past, present, and future. It is fluid and out of the box in how it operates. This can result in struggling to discern what is more inspiring or interesting than other things. With an open head, the pressure to know can make people feel disconnected to the rest of their design. There is no natural way of thinking about things or entering into a conversation with another person. Focusing can be a challenge, especially with social media, the twenty-four-seven news cycle, and the plethora of information available. This can result in not knowing what to think about, overconsuming information, disconnecting from their intellect, and feeling anxiety or fear around thinking.

When healthy, the open head has a boundless capacity for wisdom and learns to understand the mental pressure to know and discern what is inspiring to them based on their strategy and authority. With time, the healthy open head center can absorb all the amplified pressure of others (since all open and undefined centers amplify the energy of others) and allow it to pass through them without identifying with it. With an open head, you will become sensitive to the nuances of it and can gauge who uses their mind effectively and who does not. You may even find yourself sensitive enough to discern hat others are thinking. You have the ability to get into the depth and explore the wonders of the mind.

Open Ajna—Those with an open ajna will struggle to organize their thoughts and have nothing fixed or reliable to attach onto when it comes to processing information in this center. This can leave those with an open ajna with a sense of helplessness and anxiety about thinking at all. Since the ajna is how we process information, this can be challenging for mind-oriented society.

On the flip side, those with an open ajna also have the pleasure of fluidity in their ability to think about a variety of theories, concepts, and insights without attachment to any of them. Through the process of discernment, you can learn to recognize what is a good thought or concept, which when provoked by the right time can help you move to the next level. Since the open ajna amplifies those, there is a depth of wisdom with respect to the not-self. The gift of the open ajna when following your strategy and authority is the ability to help others see when they are in their "not-selves."

Open Throat—While this is one of the rarest of the open centers, people with an open throat center will struggle with what to say or what to take action on. Often children with an open throat center will talk later in life. With an open throat center, you may find yourself with the wrong timing, speaking in a borrowed voice and taking action on something that is not correct for you. This results in being ignored or not heard.

If you learn to embrace the flexibility and unpredictability of your speaking, your confidence will flourish as long as you are following your strategy and authority. This center will also provide a depth of wisdom as to who is speaking authentically from their own journey.

Open Identity—If you have a completely open identity center, you may be left feeling as though there aren't any clear parameters or guardrails as to who you are and your purpose in life. You can feel afloat and unsure of yourself, and therefore, you outsource your direction to others, with hopes that if you allow others to direct and guide you, you will finally feel lovable. This, of course, leaves you open and vulnerable to being influenced and/or manipulated by others. You give away your authority and will no longer be able to live your potential until you take it back.

As you become comfortable with the openness of your design and learn your strategy and authority, you will discover your sense of direction, your purpose, and your unique being. You have a broad experience and comprehension of the nature of being, self-love, and how we are meant to move through life.

Open Heart—With an open heart center, you will naturally struggle to understand your worthiness, how to measure what is worthy, and what you need to do in order to be worthy. You will often oscillate between having an extreme sense of worth and importance and feeling no worth at all a.k.a. worthless. This will often rear its head as a lack of self-esteem and an overwhelming sense of inadequacy. You can be particularly susceptible to being manipulated or controlled by others and can often believe in this or that extreme propaganda.

When healthy, you are a beacon of trustworthiness when it comes to the material plane, especially concerning one's word, money, and personal power. Your wisdom shines when you realize you have nothing to prove and can rely on your strategy and authority to provide for you.

Open Spleen—With an open spleen, you can oscillate between feeling no fear at all and/or being overwhelmed by fear. We are all designed to have a healthy level of fear in order to stay alive. With this open center, you can lose that connection with fear (the healthy kind that keeps you alive) and take extreme risks or be so frozen by fear that you are insecure and fear everything. You may struggle to know what to be afraid of, or you may be fearless to the point of foolishness and risk.

When healthy, the open spleen has a depth of instinctual and intuitive intelligence vibrating through this center. This includes the ways our values and our entrepreneurial endeavors nurture, protect, and ensure the survival of our species and offspring and keep our society growing.

Open Sacral—Those with an open sacral struggle to understand what to do with its energy. You will often find your energy scattered all over the place, drawn to many different things, then you will overexert yourself to the point of complete exhaustion from activity and overwhelm before it crashes and stops.

When healthy, this center can filter the life force energy of the sacral and discern what a good use for this energy would be. You can then express or describe the many qualities this unique energy brings to humanity. Many with an open sacral have a fascination with understanding who we are and why we are here. The open sacral gives us a depth of wisdom and insight into the nature of our being.

Open Solar Plexus—With the open emotional solar plexus, there is a challenge of filtering and connecting to the often potent and powerful emotional energy. Those with an open solar plexus can become confused by what they are "feeling" and not know how to interpret it. You can often lose or be consumed by what to desire and when to be sensitive or passionate, and you may struggle to connect with other people's moods.

With an open solar plexus, you might feel like something is wrong with you emotionally. The gift of the open solar plexus is that you have the wisdom to understand, observe, and be deeply empathetic to the emotional waves. You can experience them at their purest state without attaching to them, identifying with them, or having a prejudice about them. You are the ultimate empath when your solar plexus is healthy as you amplify the "emotions" of those around you.

Open Root—You will be able to experience the breadth of the pressure to do of the root from the stillness of focus to hyperactivity and everything in between. When you are out of congruence with your strategy and authority, you will often struggle with the amplified adrenal pressure of the root and the accompanying mental pressure to push you through life often making the wrong decisions. You speed up, say yes, hustle, and hurry through life so that you can be free of the pressure to do. You become conditioned to believe this is the way because you take in the root energy of others and amplify. Burnout often results from this pressure felt in the open root.

We live in a fast-paced world, and this amplified pressure of the open root center can be intense. Learning to recognize this pressure is key to having a healthy root. This amplified pressure to do is not yours. Learning to use this energy productivity in congruence with your strategy and authority is key. Your system will struggle to keep up with this fast-paced, pressure-filled way of life. Nature can offer a place of peace for those with an open root. It is a buffer zone from the demands of the world we live in.

Learn to allow the pressure to pass through you and witness it—it's not your own—and allow yourself to reconnect with a healthy pressure within yourself. Learning to find the balance of the momentum that moves life forward and the pressure to be still is key. Once you have found this balance, you will find that sense of peace and wisdom with the clarity to see and evaluate the nature and effects of this fundamental yet often overwhelming stress on others and our society.

Embracing Your Defined & Undefined Centers

One of the best suggestions I have in working with these centers is to pick one defined center and one undefined center and get to know the energy of them. Learn to know the energy that comes off of those centers. Learn the highs and the lows. Learn the personality that lives in those centers. Peel back the layers and get to know who you are in those centers.

SHOULDING YOURSELF AND THE NOT-SELF OF THE MIND IN BUSINESS

Have you ever thought, *Oh I should do that*? Or *I should do this*? I have been hearing it more and more, with clients, colleagues, and on social media. The reality is I'm guilty of "shoulding myself" from time to time as well. The more I pay attention, the more I hear it in different iterations as well, like "This makes sense" or my personal favorite: "On paper this looks great."

When I take a step back to think about what "shoulding" actually is, especially through the lens of Human Design, it is the not-self of the undefined and open centers and the low expression of our defined centers.

The shoulding shows up in our

- Marketing and keeping up with the latest trends like TikTok or Instagram Reels
- Sales, selling systems, and tools
- Need to try the new thing or tool, a.k.a. glittery object syndrome
- Offers and business model trends
- Idea of what "success" is
- Working hours

- Pricing
- Time frame to respond

If we examine our "shoulding" through the lens of Human Design, this is the not-self of the mind. The not-self of the mind is the spokesperson or mental monologue of the mind when we are out of congruence with one of our centers or with our strategy and authority. In the Human Design chart, there are several places where we can be in the not-self or low expression; for example, the following:

- With our type—Projector—bitterness & resentment; Manifestor— anger & shame; Manifesting Generator—frustration & anger; Generator—frustration; and Reflector—disappointment.
- And with the nine centers—head, ajna, throat, identity, heart, solar plexus, spleen, sacral, and root.

For this discussion on shoulding and the not-self of the mind in business, we are going to stick with the not-self of the centers. There are three ways centers show up in the Human Design chart: (1) defined—colored in, (2) undefined— white with only gates, and (3) open—no gates. Within each center, there is a polarity and a dichotomy. The high expression and the low expression, particularly with the undefined centers (the white ones). The undefined centers are the places where we take on conditioning and end up in the not-self. Of which, the mind is the not-self spokesperson of these centers or the voice of the "should." The conditioning comes from friends, family, coaches, those around us, society, cultural norms, social media, and more. When we are in the "not-self," we are out of congruence with our strategy and authority. The not-self of the mind is a tricky thing because it wants to logic us. Its sole purpose is to keep us alive. The mind, through the lens of Human Design, is here to be in service of others. It is not here to be used as a decision-making tool for us to operate on ourselves. That is what our strategy and authority is for.

The mind is rational, reasonable, sensemaking, and logical. It yearns to do the thing or things that make the most sense based on what we have seen, read about, or experienced. The mind operates from a place of fear and pressure. It is primitive in this sense even though it is very powerful (and convincing). For many of us, we live in the place of "if this makes sense, then it must be correct for me." I know I have operated in this way in the past even when my gut was screaming for me to go in a different direction. The challenge with this is that our gut, intuition, or inner knowing will often nudge us to do x and our mind "logics" us out of those decisions.

When we leverage Human Design as a tool, we rely on our authority for our decision-making process rather than the logic of our mind, especially when it comes to our business. Our strategy depends on what energy type we are: Projector—wait for the invitation/recognition; Generator—respond/know thyself; Manifesting Generator—visualize, respond & then inform; Manifestor—initiate/inform; and Reflector—wait a lunar cycle.

Part of the reason I believe this to be so important, especially for my fellow entrepreneurs, is because when we are out of congruence, we aren't in the highest expression of ourselves. We will struggle to reach the full potential of who we are when we are in the not-self. The reality is when we leverage Human Design as a tool to look at where we are out of congruence, it is because we have gotten lost somewhere along the way. We have fallen off track with our strategy and authority. We have given our power away. We've outsourced our thinking. Ultimately leaving us in a place where we didn't expect to be. We have taken on conditioning and carrying something that is not ours. In our undefined centers, we can take on layers and layers of conditioning along the way and we lose ourselves. We lose sight of our lighthouse.

I love using the lighthouse here as a metaphor because if you think of what a lighthouse does it stands tall shining its light. Think of your Human Design blueprint as a lighthouse and the light shining round and round from the lighthouse as your strategy and authority. When we take on layers and layers of conditioning, we can get pulled out to sea and lose sight of our light. We lose sight of where we are, and we have to come back home again to ourselves.

The mind and the not-self of the mind are here to keep us alive, but they are not here to help us live out the fullest expression of our being. The mind is not here to help us fuel our passions and spark a fire within us. The mind is not for fulfilling your purpose. It is literally here for survival. So when we use our mind for decision-making, we betray our future selves. We betray our bigger purpose. We betray the impact we as entrepreneurs want to make. However, our minds are brilliant tools when they are in service of the other. The mind is simply not here to operate on itself. Imagine if you broke your arm and you needed surgery. You wouldn't try to operate on yourself. Next time your mind attempts to take over your strategy and authority think of this as operating on yourself. It's not the best idea.

Now let's get back to the centers . . . For each of the centers, the not-self of the mind, the "shoulding," is going to show up in a different way. For example:

With the Head
- "I should be further along."
- "I should know more."
- "I should be able to figure this out."
- "I should get to work, but I'll just spend five more minutes scrolling."

With the Ajna
- "I should do this because this is what is normal/typical/standard for my industry."
- "I shouldn't do this because people will think I'm weird."
- "I should do this because this is what's expected of me in my industry."
- "I should know what to do next."

With the Throat
- "I should be showing up online and getting more visible."
- "I should be making TikToks or Instagram Reels or *insert trend here*."
- "I should be getting more likes/engagement/interaction."
- "I shouldn't bother showing up online; no one sees my stuff anyway."
- "I should do this podcast interview because it's going to get me exposure."

With the Identity

- "I should do it this way because x is doing it that way."
- "I should have a five-year plan for my business."
- "I should know what my purpose/strengths/passions/direction are."
- "I should love what I do because it's my business but . . ."
- "I shouldn't change direction/pivot because . . ."

With the Heart

- "I should raise my prices."
- "I should try this new thing/tech/trend because I don't want to miss out."
- "I should join this program because that is *the* thing that will change the game for me."
- "I should do this thing because then they will finally see my worth/how valuable I am."

With the Solar Plexus

- "I should be happy."
- "I should keep doing this because it is easy even though I hate it."
- "I should go this route because I don't want to waste all the effort I put in."
- "I should go this route because I don't want to upset anyone or let my team/people down."
- "I should talk to x because I'm not happy, but it's easier just to do it myself."

With the Spleen

- "I should show up, but I'm afraid I don't know enough/I'm not expert enough."
- "I should do x because Sarah does it that way, and I fear if I don't do it that way, I won't be successful."
- "I should pivot my business, but I'm just going to keep holding on because I'm afraid of _____."
- "I should do x, but I'm afraid/overwhelmed/have anxiety about doing x because I might fail/be successful/have to let go."

- "I should do this now instead of later because I fear I will _____."

With the Sacral
- "I should do a course and an evergreen product and a _____ and a _____ (all the things)."
- "I should keep working even though I'm exhausted."
- "I should be working since it is "work hours.""
- "I should set better boundaries with my clients but _____."
- "I should stay focused on my goals, but I fear I'm going to miss out if I don't say yes/do this thing."

With the Root
- "I should hurry up because I'm behind."
- "I should do this because x is already doing it, and I have to keep up."
- "I should do _____ even though I'm already stressed."
- "I should do this because my clients/family/friends/person needs me."
- "I should try this new thing even though it might sabotage this other thing I'm working on."
- "I should be able to get past this block/level/limiting belief. What is wrong with me?"

When I hear that logic of the mind, that sensemaking, it is often a sign that the person is in their not-self. They are "shoulding" themselves with reasons why they should do this or that. Although intuitively, they might not necessarily agree with their "shoulding."

In Human Design, we rely on strategy and authority for our decision-making process. For example, I'm a Projector with emotional authority. For me, I first have to wait for the invitation and receive recognition from the other, then I have to ride the highs and lows of my emotional wave and get to an emotional neutral. Once I am at that neutral, I can then discern whether that is the right decision for me.

I might be recognized to do this thing, but then I also have to ride my emotional wave to discern whether this actually is the right thing for me to do. I recently got invited to write a chapter for a book. It is with a great publisher, and I got the invite and recognition on why I would be the right expert and writer. So I can enter into this knowing I followed my strategy of waiting for the invitation and recognition.

Now I have to lean into my emotional wave to discern whether I actually want to do this. Is the timing right? Is this a yes for me? I caught myself in the process of this "shoulding." "I should do this because, you know, this is going to help get me exposure"—the not-self of the throat. "I should do this because it's going to position me as an expert"—the not-self of the identity center. "I should do this because the Human Design world is growing so fast, and I have to keep up"—the not-self of the root center.

All of these shoulds kept coming up, and I had to get out of my not-self thinking and into my authority. I knew it was the right thing for me, and I had 75 percent buy-in; however, I wanted to make sure the timing was right and that I could follow through on it. Ultimately, I said yes, but I honored the highs and lows of my emotional wave before I committed.

For each type, there is a strategy and an authority. Each authority corresponds to one of the centers in the body. When we are in congruence with our strategy and authority, the authority is being leveraged to make decisions instead of the mind. When we are shoulding and logic-ing and sensemaking, we are in the not-self of the mind in one of our centers. My goal in sharing all of this with you is that you can begin to recognize this in yourself with more ease, less resistance, and more quickly.

When you leverage your mind for decision-making instead of your authority, you will often find yourself in frustration, anger, resentment, or overwhelm. The mind is simply here to be in service of others and keep you alive from a primal survival level. It will always lead you astray in expressing the highest version of yourself.

Ultimately what happens when we use our minds in service of our decision-making in our businesses is that it becomes sort of a huge problem. Because one decision made by the mind, followed by another and another and another leads us out to sea where we can no longer see the light of our lighthouse. Instead, we can lean into the innate inner knowing of our intuition, our gut response, our bodies, which is ultimately our authority. Our bodies hold the truth of what is best for us, not the shoulding or logic-ing or sensemaking of the mind. Just because something looks good on paper doesn't mean that it is actually what sparks our passion and drive. That logic and shoulding is not who you are. It is simply how you are experiencing the world based on the conditioning you have taken on. That baggage, conditioning, not-self—whatever you want to call it. The layers you are carrying that are not yours. You can put them down. You can free yourself from the weight of conditioning with a bit of work.

It's incredibly freeing once you put it down. I've been studying Human Design for three years now and living in congruence with my strategy and authority. I notice now with so much more speed when I am shoulding myself and when I'm out of congruence. That is because I've gotten to know myself better. I've gotten to know where I tend to take on conditioning, and I've been working through peeling back all the layers of stuff that are not mine. Human Design has given me a framework for my intuition and language for understanding my uniqueness and a process for how I'm best to interact with the world.

This work takes time. It takes time to reestablish trust with our bodies when we have been relying on our minds for years. It takes time, repetition, and a bit of belief in listening to our authority instead of our minds. In our culture, we are programmed to rely on our minds from a very early age. You wouldn't go to the gym for the first time in years and expect to be able to deadlift 250 pounds. The same goes for trusting your authority (and strategy). Start with small decisions first. Look back on your past lived experiences when things have worked out (or haven't) and go step by step through what happened. Did you rely on your mind? Or did you trust your gut?

I encourage you to lean into that inner nudge, that voice within that spark, that passion, that fire, that thing you want to do that doesn't make sense because, ultimately, that's probably the right thing for you. I invite you to lean in: lean into the knowing, lean into the nudge, lean into the spark, lean into the intuition because what would happen if, instead of saying, "I should follow this blueprint because blah, blah, blah," we blazed the trail? What if we did things on our own terms and followed the thing that didn't make sense?

What if instead we just completely imagined a new business model or a new way to do things or a better way to serve our clients? What if we just put down the shoulds and really embraced the possibilities? The possibility we can create the life that we want to create and the business that we want to create on our own terms, when we stay true to who we are.

KNOW, EMBODY, BECOME.

When I teach, I always offer a lot of depth. The reason I offer a lot of depth is twofold: (1) Human Design has a great deal of depth to it, and (2) depth offers the learner the ability to discern what resonates with them. From my experience in teaching and learning Human Design, I have found certain things stick with us depending upon where we are in our journey. We may, in fact, hear that same thing later on and it resonates differently.

Depth offers us the option to really dig into the subject and the knowing. I firmly believe that when we offer our clients depth (and let's be honest, they are craving and yearning for it), there is a higher potential for embodying that knowledge and actually making a transformation.

In the HD In the Wild Program, I share a deeper look into this process which I call Know, Embody, Become. Much of the work I do with clients is peeling back their layers of conditioning as they take on the new Human Design knowledge in order to hold space for others.

The reality is most of what is offered on the internet is surface level. It treats the symptom, not the root. I won't go into the whys or my frustration with this, but the reality is that it is shallow.

In order to create transformation and change (besides the obvious—being willing), we must also have a depth of knowledge and knowing in order to actually trust that which we cannot see yet. This calms and quiets the not-self of our mind (although it still may be chatty) because it makes sense. We logic it, which is what the mind needs. Knowledge, Depth, Answers.

From there, we can then spot this in the real world and have an awareness, or as I like to say, we can recognize that there is a flag on the field of our life (like in American football with penalty flags). Let's say, for example, you are experiencing FOMO (fear of missing out) for buying a new course. When we have an awareness that we are looking outside ourselves for yet another solution, we can then recognize that we are unaligned with who we are meant to be. Through the lens of Human Design, this works for *all* of the not-self themes and every time we "should" ourselves. With awareness, we can recognize with more ease (and more quickly) when we are giving our power away, when we aren't using our voice, when we have outsourced our decision-making, or when we are experiencing frustration, anger, overwhelm, disappointment, or bitterness. We have to reckon with this part of ourselves that was never ours.

When we have awareness, we can then dig into the question: what is the story that I am telling myself here? This is how we get to the root of the symptom—by digging into what we are telling ourselves. What beliefs, stories, cultural norms, and conditioning are there? Do we like this story? Is it our story or belief? Or is it what we believe we should do? If we were to throw out the rules, what would we actually believe? What would our story actually be? What do we desire to do? Then we can take that story and its lesson forward with us, through a new lens.

Through this lesson, we can then begin to *embody* that which we desire. We can rewrite the story we have told ourselves for months or weeks or even years. We can begin to embody a version of ourselves that is more in congruence with who we are. We can embody a new story. A new way of being that comes with more ease. This embodiment happens over time . . . and as we begin to embody, we bring in more space and grace, more flow, more joy, and more success in both life and biz.

Then we inhabit a new way of being as we fully integrate the new story. We begin to move differently; we are more grounded, more mindful, more at ease in our bodies. This is often where we must truly reckon with that part of ourselves that was never really ours to begin with. This is where the self-doubt and the questioning come into play because self-doubt clings to us, not wanting to let go of what was so that we can truly become.

And only once we inhabit that new way of being, when we let go and begin again, then and only then can we become. As we become, we can shed the layers that kept us believing old stories. Stories that kept us stuck. Stories that held us back. Stories that no longer serve us.

The reality is, this process happens over and over again on the way to becoming. It is not a quick fix or an overnight change. It is something we must lean into. It is something to allow. It is something that transforms us. It requires us to reckon with who we think we are and who we truly are at our core. It is letting go and holding on. It is deep work. It is catalytic work. It is vulnerable work.

I have personally cycled through this more times than I can even count since learning my Human Design back in 2019. This process of becoming requires time, willingness, and letting go. It requires vulnerability, resilience, and patience. It requires you to look at yourself and the stories you have told yourself through different lenses. It requires space and grace. It requires understanding, depth, and most importantly, *trust*. If you'd like to dig deeper into this process, check out the blog on my website jamielpalmer.com.

Know, Embody, Become Process
with my Human Design in Business Work

Know — Depth — Should'ing — Aware — Story — Embody — Reckon — Lesson — Inhabit — Become

Jamie Palmer

Part 2—
Human Design for Business

DISCERNING YOUR BUSINESS CONTAINER & CLIENT

L et's set the scene…

You've gleaned more insight into who you are as a person and how you are designed to operate. We are now going to take that knowing, those insights, and the trust we are building with ourselves and apply them to our businesses. To build a business based on who we are as a human, how we are designed to operate, and what brings us joy, we are going to imagine and step on the path to creating a better future for ourselves. One that throws out the rules of what we "should do" or "how it's always been done." Or the "that's not how you launch" or "do business."

We are going to reimagine a future where we tap into our truth, our design, and our insights to discern what is best for us. With each moment we tap into, our inner knowing grows stronger, wiser, more resilient, and more trustworthy. We become more confident. Our back stands taller. We rise up. We become who we've always wanted to be. We say yes to ourselves. We say yes to the lives we want to create. We don't question our truth, and we don't let our monkey minds take over. We have become aware of when we get carried away and gently pull ourselves back into congruence with grace. We each have the power within us to shine, to know, to trust. It is simply a matter of continuing to cultivate that power, knowing, and trust over time.

The Reality of the Online Space Today

There is a plague in the online business space, and this plague is intended to keep you stuck on a hamster wheel or treadmill of hustle, business "meh," and in general, feeling like you can't keep up. The reason this plague is so dominant is because it ties into our innate desires and motivations, our emotions, and our need for community. It is the need to fit in, to try something, to not miss out, to "be better, build bigger," etc. It tugs at our heartstrings, *and* it keeps many of us stuck, doing many things, but not very well.

What is this plague? This plague is the plague of juggling. Of trying something once and then not following through. It is the plague of creating a course, launching it once, and then starting from scratch again. It is the plague of *un*-sticktoitiveness. It is the plague of this next best thing will be the thing that solves your problem. It is the plague that you are not enough. It is a plague of the mind, and it plays tricks on us. The not-self of the mind takes over, and we end up in this place where we've given away ourselves, our power, and what we know to be right.

We've outsourced our thinking and our decision-making to others without considering what feels good to us, what is correct for the lifestyle that we want to have, or where we want to be in a year.

The reality is this plague is littered all over the online world . . . in systems and processes, in new methods and trends, in doing one new course and then another new membership and program, and it keeps you stuck.

I want you to stop and think for a moment about some of your favorite companies and businesses. Go back to their beginnings. Look at the history of their company. They did one thing and they did it really well and they sold you into a mission, a lifestyle, and/or a transformation. One that lit you up inside. One that made you feel really, really good, and for the most part, they did it *really* well. Some examples of this are Spanx, Coca-Cola, Zappos, TOMS, B-School, James Clear, and so many more.

There is a time and a place to diversify and grow, and there is a time and a place to simplify, to *focus*.

I strongly believe most entrepreneurs diversify before they have even given themselves a chance to be successful. They launch something one time, and it goes OK, and then they move on to whatever next best thing has come along.

Maybe they go back and launch that thing again, but more often than not, it sits, collecting dust, never to be seen in the world again.

This is in part due to the industry and in part due to the fact that we entrepreneurs are creative people. We love to build and create. We break rules. We do things our own way. We like being the boss. We like making something from nothing. We like doing all the things to make something, but when it comes time to market it and sell it . . . most of us struggle. We much prefer to create than to market and sell. Probably in part due to the fact that with selling comes rejection, which is one of our primal fears, to be rejected. The problem, however, is this thinking is also keeping us stuck, repeating the same cycle over and over again.

Let me be clear: I am not suggesting you only create and do one thing for the rest of your career. I'm simply suggesting that you *focus* rather than follow glittery object syndrome down the rabbit hole of scrapping what you just created and doing something entirely different. Creating new content, creating a new sales page, creating new emails and social media and workbooks, and the list goes on and on.

I'm suggesting you create one program, you systematize it, you put the support systems in place, you truly build it out, *and* you actually market it. Radical I know, but think about the possibility.

What I'm suggesting here is to take one container, for one year, and you nurture it. You cultivate it. You tweak it. You give it life. You feed it. You do what you need to do in order to create an ecosystem so that it can thrive. *You follow one course until successful.*

Now this is often the point where I'm met with resistance . . .

"But, Jam, what about the student who just went through my x program? I need to have something for them." Maybe, or you could offer them to go through your container again at a bit of a lower price point. Or maybe you create a referral relationship to get paid to support them in the next step.

"But, Jam, I'm a Manifesting Generator and that sounds so boring to me." Or, well, let's get you as the expert in a couple of different groups where you can get paid to be your multipassionate self while you focus on growing one container, or you take all that energy and funnel it into creative ways to grow your business.

"But, Jam, aren't people going to get sick of me promoting the same thing?" You'd be surprised at how many times you need to say something before someone actually takes action and moves forward, plus more often than not it takes time to grow a business.

"But, Jam, what if I don't like the business model I chose, and now I'm stuck with it?" Great! We have some data points to make some decisions to tweak and hone the program because the reality is the content will stay the same, but the delivery and support with clients can change. I can't tell you how many times I've tweaked and honed my Business Ecosystem Builders program.

"But, Jam, this can't possibly work for me because _____ (insert some excuse around how their business is different)." The reality is all of our businesses are different *and* most of us aren't great at finishing. We love the excitement of starting something new, but when we have to tweak something or hone it, it's not nearly as sexy or exciting. When we have to sit and look at data and our messaging and take a good hard look at what's not working, it's uncomfortable.

The work of building a business is by nature uncomfortable work. If your business is growing, you will almost always be uncomfortable because the tide is always shifting. It's our ability to embrace this discomfort and trust our inner knowing and the shining of our lighthouse to guide us back home to ourselves again and again that makes us successful.

What I am proposing is this: give yourself one year to build out one amazing container and maybe a few ancillary products. Give it your all to tweak it and hone it and market it and show up for it. Give it the effort it deserves. That you deserve. Don't let the distractions or the trends pull you into the undercurrent. Follow the path you laid, and you might just be surprised where you end up.

CONSIDERATIONS FOR
BUSINESS MODELS

When thinking about the perfect business model for you, you need to consider:

For the Business	*For the Human*
Profitability	Type
Marketing Volume	Profile
Consistency	Authority
Sales Volume	Lifestyles
Deliverables	Goals

Business Design with Human Design

BUSINESS MODEL TYPES

TYPE I

1:1 MODEL

This model is a great place to start in your business. It's also a great place to start if you have a really high level of expertise.

ADVANTAGES

- *Charge a premium*
- *High level of expertise*
- *Great starting off place for all types*
- *Low investment to get started*

PITFALLS

- *Trading dollars for hours*
- *Often no offer in place*
- *Limit to the amount of money you can make*

IDEAL FOR

- *All types & profiles, but Projectors will burn out quickly here.*
- *If you have a Line 2 in your profile you may always want to work this way*

Business Design with Human Design

BUSINESS MODEL TYPES
TYPE II

THE AGENCY / SERVICE PROVIDER MODEL

This model is great for people who like to lead and manage teams and create systems and delivery processes.

ADVANTAGES

- *Charge a premium*
- *High level of expertise*
- *Can rely on others to do deliverables in the business*
- *Lots of room for growth*
- *Requires great leadership*
- *Easy to build off of relationships/referrals*

PITFALLS

- *Managing lots of people both internally & externally*
- *Grow only as fast as you can build a team*
- *People as a process (overhead)*
- *Lots of people expense*

IDEAL FOR

- *Projectors can oscillate between the different team members— see what is broken and what needs to be fixed.*
- *Lines 4 & 6 will thrive here as well*
- *Generators will do well here since there is a lot of doing and responding*

BUSINESS MODEL TYPES
TYPE III

THE RETREAT/EVENT MODEL

With this model, you build your business simply by doing retreats and in-person events. This is great if you love spending time with people and bringing people together.

ADVANTAGES

- *Lots of energy in a short period of time*
- *Hig -level of creativity*
- *Love creating experiences*

PITFALLS

- *High output of energy for a short period of time*
- *Location / time / event-based, i.e,. one per year*
- *Limit to the number of people you can manage at an event*

IDEAL FOR

- *Manifestors & Manifesting Generators*
- *Great for people who like to get in and get out with people*
- *Good way for Line 6 to share their amazing gifts with the world.*

Business Design with Human Design

BUSINESS MODEL TYPES
TYPE IV

THE LOW-TICKET MODEL

This model has to be high in volume to be profitable. Usually, it's driving people to a higher ticket. Low-ticket is priced under $250.

ADVANTAGES

- *High Volume , Low Price*
- *Low amount of client interactions*
- *Great for people who like to create/spend time creating*
- *Marketing is a must*
- *Passive income with marketing effort*

PITFALLS

- *Lots of customer service*
- *Multiple low ticket offers*
- *Needs lots of traffic to create conversions*
- *Limit to the amount of money you can make*

IDEAL FOR

- *Line 1, 2, 5, 6 (phase 2)*
- *Go off and create*
- *Enjoy showing up online*

Business Design with Human Design

BUSINESS MODEL TYPES
TYPE V

THE MID-TICKET MODEL

This model is great if you do a whole bunch of work, get something off the ground and then choose not to work for a while. Anywhere from $300 to $2000.

ADVANTAGES

- *Medium volume*
- *Usually sold through launch—bursts of effort, periods of rest*
- *Growing audience is key to continued success*
- *Typically committed to a group of people for a period of time*
- *Definitive Start / Stop*
- *Typically build once and then good*

PITFALLS

- *Launch burnout*
- *Usually need multiple offers to keep clients on your journey*
- *Can require a fair amount of customer service*
- *Can't control who enrolls - Trust you build an audience*
- *Launching is an art and science and can be tricky*
- *Periods of ebb and flow*

IDEAL FOR

- *Most types and profiles, especially 4*
- *Design this offer around how you like to show up*
- *If you like launching (can be exhausting for some)*
- *Like working with groups for a period of time and then moving on*

Business Design with Human Design

BUSINESS MODEL TYPES
TYPE VI

THE HIGH-TICKET & MASTERMIND MODEL

For this model to work, you have to establish yourself as an expert and really plant your flag.

ADVANTAGES

- *Charge a premium for a premium experience*
- *High level of expertise*
- *Work with the same people over time*
- *Deeply want to support people*
- *Selective about whom you work with*

PITFALLS

- *Takes time to grow*
- *Not for everyone*
- *Requires immense consistency; consistently showing up to provide support*

IDEAL FOR

- *Ideal for 1, 3, 4, 6 & Projectors who bounce from person to person*
- *Consistent energy*
- *People who like to coordinate other people—think of being the mayor*
- *People who can consistently show up within a specific container*
- *Someone who likes to go deep with a few people*

Business Design with Human Design

BUSINESS MODEL TYPES
TYPE VII

THE MEMBERSHIP MODEL

This model is for people who like consistent income and don't necessarily want a big influx of money a few times a year. This model can live on the back of a low-ticket offer or a mid-ticket offer, or it can be a standalone model.

ADVANTAGES

- *High volume (in most instances)*
- *Limited interaction with people*
- *Consistent audience buildings*
- *Can create consistently*

PITFALLS

- *Relentless consistency is key to success—marketing perspective*
- *Often no offer in place*
- *Lots of customer service*

IDEAL FOR

- *People who like to consistently create, do, and build*
- *Great for generators*
- *Line 1, 5, 6*
- *Like creating community and a tribe*

Business Design with Human Design

BUSINESS MODEL TYPES
TYPE VIII

THE BOOK/SELF-STUDY MODEL

This model is great for introverts who want to create content behind the scenes, put it online, market it, and get people to buy it passively.

ADVANTAGES

- *Lots of freedom*
- *Very limited people interaction*
- *Audience building through the lens of a book*
- *Great to pair with other models*

PITFALLS

- *Large time investment*
- *Can be lonely*
- *Audience building*

IDEAL FOR

- *People who take the initiative*
- *People who are self-motivated*
- *Like to create*
- *Line 1, 2, 5, manifestors*

Business Design with Human Design

BUSINESS MODEL TYPES
TYPE IX

THE ECOMMERCE MODEL

This business model is very people- and process-driven. It's all about delivery systems and fulfillment.

ADVANTAGES

- *Only need to build an audience*
- *No or very limited client interactions*
- *Solve a problem for the marketplace*
- *Low barrier to entry*

PITFALLS

- *Lots of customer support/service*
- *High investment to get started (potentially)*
- *Can be low profitability based on each product*
- *Managing inventory*
- *Lots of variables outside of your control, e.g., shipping*

IDEAL FOR

- *Passionate introverts*
- *Patient and not easily influenced by outside factors*
- *Enjoy building a team and working with the same people*

How to Pick Your Business Model and Container

Now that I've shared all of the containers and some recommendations, I want to add a caveat here: I am simply making recommendations based on my experience of working with entrepreneurs. You must follow your own strategy, authority, and inner knowing as to what is correct for you.

I think picking our business model or container is one of the first places we give our power away as entrepreneurs. We think to ourselves, *Well if it worked for x, it'll work for me.* Or *If it's not broken, why fix it.* This thinking makes me a bit annoyed and the reason is that it fails to take into account what you want. How you want to show up in the world. The lifestyle you want to create. How you want to support clients.

And for those of you who are quietly thinking, *Oh, it's not possible to build a big company without working lots of hours . . .* I see you and I challenge your thinking. I have worked with dozens if not hundreds of clients at this point who have built a business around who they are and how many hours they want to show up.

Now let's be clear: I'm not promising every week is going to be sunshine and rainbows. There will be seasons where you need to put in more work and more hours to create a foundation your future self will thank you for, and once that foundation is in place, you can use that as a platform to keep growing and building from.

I'll use my client Sarah as an example. She's a former health coach turned business coach for health coaches. Over the last five years in our work together, she has slowly built two different containers to support clients, and her annual revenue has been over $500K per year. Within the next year or two, we project she will break that one million dollar mark. She is a Projector who works about twenty-five hours a week and spends of the rest of her time outdoors. She typically takes an entire month off to go on vacation at least once per year and continues to grow her business by focusing on the fundamentals. The entire premise for our work together was to build a minimalist business. While, of course, this is not for everyone, this is what works for her.

But all of this started because she defined what she wanted, defined how she wanted to show up, and said no to everything that wasn't that. Of course, there were a few ups and downs along the way, which is to be expected, but for the most part, she enjoys three-day weekends, skis almost daily, and works four or five hours a day.

So when you think about your days, your weeks, your months, and the lifestyle you want to cultivate, what do *you* want? How do you want to show up and support clients? How many hours a day do you want to work? What do you want your week to look like?

Take some time to contemplate and imagine what that looks like for you. There is no idea too unrealistic or too big or too little. The choice is yours and yours alone. Tap into your strategy and authority. Tap into you and write it down. Use the workbook to contemplate, write, and discern what you want. Not what's best for the client. What's best for you. Because the client will get what's best for them when you put yourself first.

Now Let's Talk Ideal Client & Transformation

I sometimes wonder if we get the typical methodology wrong with identifying our ideal clients. Perhaps wrong is a strong word, but stick with me here because this isn't the typical way we are taught to think about our ideal clients.

The typical way is that this person is within this age bracket, and here are these demographics—the car they drive, the fears they have, their motives, and these things that unite them together but within this particular space in time. I can't tell you how many clients I've worked with over the years who have had mothers of school-age children as their ideal clients. Now I'm not saying we don't use this technique; in fact, I'm going to share with you my human exercise in the workbook, and what I'm suggesting here is we dig deeper.

A great example of this is a retail store as it is very obvious. They carefully curate the styles they select to be sold each season based on age, race, gender, class, location, etc. They shout his on social media through the models wearing their outfits, the photos showcasing their clothes, the language they use, and so on. The same goes for the digital business world.

And I'm not saying this doesn't work. It does, and in some industries, it is entirely necessary, *but* I also believe for experts, creators, and coaches, there may, in fact, be a better way.

What if, instead, we looked at it from the perspective of the transformation that we get the clients as a result of their work with us. Let me elaborate a bit . . .

With my most recent HD Your Biz™ launch, the vibrant thread I wove through all the content was this idea of bringing more joy to your life and business, to tuning up the definition in your business, to creating a business that sparked more joy. Ultimately, with the goal of creating a business that was more in congruence with who you are as a person.

In my content leading up to the launch, I shared personal experiences from my own business and spoke to the near constant resistance you can face as a business owner. I talked about the struggle of pivoting and how nice it would have been to get my business "right" in the first place. All of these are values I live by without saying, "Here are my values."

The result was that fifty-seven incredible souls said yes. It is *the* most diverse group I've ever worked with. People from all over the world. In all stages of business. At every age (twenty-something to almost eighty). In all phases of life. All of them are looking to tune up the definition in their life and business.

My belief is this: when we only think of our ideal client through the lens of demographics, fears, and motivations, we are missing the unifying piece. We limit ourselves. We miss the boat of the impact we are trying to make in the world. We miss many of the people we intend to serve simply because they don't believe we are speaking to them.

We need to zoom out and speak to the transformation they are yearning to get. The values that they live by. The things that spark joy or a fire in their soul. We need to universalize without losing our personality and speak in the words our clients use. We've got to embody it. We've got to help them see the light of hope. I call this the Transformation Promise. You can look to your profile, type, and defined centers to shine a light on what your transformation promise may be.

For example, as a 3/5 Projector, I am here to disrupt the way things have always been done and show people a new way by challenging the status quo.

I want you to think about it for a moment. What is the unifying piece that ties together the transformation you help your clients get? It might be helpful to go back establish some core values as guiding principles. It might be helpful to create a mission statement, or for some it might simply pop into your head.

The reality is when we have this transformation in place, it is the vibrant thread that weaves together everything we do and hope to achieve. It provides hope, sparks confidence, and helps us see we aren't alone. The thing is . . . this is much easier said than it is done. That is why I am planting the seed of this here. This may take time to develop and cultivate. It may take time to hone, to get the language just right, or to get the message to land.

Which is also why I recommend you work through the human exercises in the workbook to help you gain clarity on who you serve.

The Marketer vs. the Expert

I think it is important to mention here that often, especially with the clients I support, people get stuck. They often say things like, "So and So who is not nearly as experienced as I am is making ten times more than I am." Or "I don't understand why they are so successful; they aren't really teaching anything new. My program is so much more in-depth."

If you have ever found yourself saying any iteration of that, then keep reading. The reality is that person who isn't as experienced as you, who isn't as discerning, who doesn't have a fully codified process, that person you are comparing yourself to and wondering why you aren't where they are, it's because they are an expert at marketing themselves. They have mastered the art of marketing. So I like to bring up this idea of the marketer vs. the expert.

The expert is someone who . . .

- speaks in tech jargon—language the ideal client can't understand or doesn't necessarily understand unless they are solution or product aware (more on that to come)
- struggles to show up with a consistent effort in their marketing, and when they do market, it often doesn't resonate
- speaks the problem they know they can solve vs. the problem the client believes they have
- isn't speaking the same language as the ideal client
- may cause eyes to glaze over out of bordom

The marketer is someone who…

- speaks in the language the ideal client uses
- isn't afraid to have a strong call to action
- asks for the sale
- speaks to the problem the ideal client believes they have
- is consistent with their marketing message and shows up

Learning to discern when and where to put your marketing hat on and when to put on your expert hat is key. Now again, what that looks like for you will differ based on your type, profile, strategy, and authority.

Let's Dive into an Example

A very common mistake online entrepreneurs make is that they constantly have their expert hat on, and it often results in them giving away free advice. It results in them literally repelling their ideal clients. The ideal client does not understand what they are talking about because of the technical jargon, or they feel overwhelmed. It's an unnatural way to sell. The reality is people love to buy but hate to be sold to. So when we are trying hard to sell our stuff, it creates resistance and tension in the relationship. It's easier for us to put our expert's hat on than to actually be a marketer or to be a salesperson.

For me and in my industry especially, I see these people who are so underqualified from an expert perspective, yet they are crushing it with sales because they are really, really good at marketing. Personally, that drives me completely bananas! I believe that if you have an awareness of when it's time to be a marketer and when it's time to be an expert, it becomes easier to oscillate back and forth between which hat it's appropriate to wear and when.

What is a marketer? A marketer is a person or a company that advertises or promotes something.

What is an expert? An expert is defined as a person who has a comprehensive and authoritative knowledge of a skill or knowledge in a particular area. You can also think of an expert as somebody who has done ten thousand hours. (The ten thousand-hour rule: it roughly takes you ten years to become a well-known expert.)

I bring this up because when you think about what it means to be an expert in marketing versus a marketer, I would contend that it comes down to understanding how your ideal client speaks about the problem that they believe they have and you have the solution for.

More often than not, there is a disconnect. Here's an example of a client of mine: a former professor turned entrepreneur. He's an amazing educator and has been in the education space for many years. He helps parents and students get organized, create systems, and create a plan for success. Unfortunately, most parents don't believe that that's what their student needs to be successful.

Most people believe that

their student just need to work harder

they don't have a great teacher

their child should be getting better grades

Those are problems parents believe they have. So, if my client were to market himself by saying, "I have a system to help your student get organized and help them accomplish more and be more successful in school," they are saying two different things.

Why? Part of that is that's him being his expert self because he knows the solution really is the underlying problem. The underlying solution is that the kid does not have a system to set them up for success.

They haven't created a habit.

They haven't established a routine.

He can't sell that to a parent, however, because that's not what the parent believes to be the problem. And so that's Steven being an expert.

As a marketer, Steven has to speak to the problem that the ideal client believes they have because it's going to be easier for him to get somebody to hit that "Buy Now" button if they're on the same page. I've been guilty of this. My clients have been guilty of this. And I still slip into this mode from time to time!

It is really easy for us to fall into that trap of putting our expert hat on by helping people come up with a solution, or just by saying, "Here's a solution, blah blah blah blah blah," and we completely lose people as a result because we're not speaking the same language.

It's as if you were speaking to somebody in French, but they only spoke German, English, or Spanish. It just isn't going to work.

As you go to market yourself, it is very important to understand who your ideal client is:

What words do they use?

What language keeps them up at night?

What motivates them?

What is status to them and all of those little intricacies?

What is it that they truly desire?

What are their beliefs around themselves, their family, and their core values?

You need to have an understanding of all of this. The better understanding you can have about your ideal client, the faster you're going to close that gap between when somebody first introduces themselves to your brand and when they become a client.

I've seen the most ridiculously talented people who I've worked with revamp their sales page and go back to expert mode instead of being a marketer. Ultimately that's great, but there's such a steep learning curve when it comes to that, that you will often lose your ideal client to somebody who's not as qualified as you.

So if you are an expert and wondering, "Why can't I just get these people to convert?" you have to ultimately bridge the gap between where that ideal client believes they are based on your research versus the language that you use.

For example, I did a big Black Friday promotion a few years back and was in research mode to get real-time feedback around what people's biggest struggles are when it comes to marketing and social media. I will use that research as part of my sales page and put it in quotations. Maybe take the most popular ones and integrate them into my marketing because that way I am speaking to that ideal client.

When I'm speaking to them, I want them to be like, "Yes, Jamie. How did you get into my brain?" and that is ultimately one of, if not *the*, most important thing you can do to get somebody to go from prospect to buyer and really bridge and close that gap.

Here are my tips on how you can understand when it is time to be an expert and when it is time to be a marketer:

As a general rule of thumb, most of your 90 to 95 percent front-facing marketing for social media can be you as a marketer.

Your sales pages can be you as a marketer.

You can be a marketer when you're speaking to a potential client, especially if they're not a referral and they're not really warmed up yet.

You can be a marketer in your nurture sequence.

You can be an expert when you are sharing some behind-the-scenes content, in your email list, for example, or when speaking with an existing client.

Your macro content can be you as an expert but sprinkled in with a marketer—a coalescence of the two. When you're doing webinars and masterclasses, that content can be sprinkled in.

Your expert self can be sprinkled in on sales calls. And then once somebody purchases from you, you can put that expert hat on twenty-four seven, especially once they have purchased your signature program. If they haven't purchased your signature program, but rather a $47 product—in my case, somebody would buy a $47 social media snapshot—there's going to be no selling, it's going to be all expertise, but I have to leave them wanting more for that next step in the client journey. There's a lot to talk about in the client journey, but you don't want to just give it all away in that one first product. You want them to move on to that next product and the next . . .

When somebody is in your signature program or your high-level offer, that's where you can put the expert cap on twenty-four seven and really get them to move on to that next level.

When you understand your ideal client really well and you can use the exact language your ideal client uses, this becomes very easy. One thing to be aware of is that for most of us entrepreneurs, our default mode is expert and that can be a real challenge. So be mindful of when you're in expert mode and when you slip back into marketer mode or vice versa.

I highly recommend reading through all your content through the lens of your ideal client. Pay attention because it's really easy to slip into expert mode! At the start of a sales call, you are in a marketing role, and then you can accidentally slip into expert mode, especially when ideal clients are asking you questions. Quickly you get wrapped up in a discussion, and then before you know it, you've given away a whole bunch of free advice.

Keep in mind when the eyes glaze over or you get the deer in the headlights look, that's when you know you've gone too far with the expert mode! You completely lost the other person or overwhelmed them because you're speaking so much tech jargon to them. It's OK to be a geek about what you do, but you have to always bring it back to that marketer, to get the ideal client to take that next step, to get them to move forward.

MARKETING

The reality is if you want to build a business, you have to actually market and sell yourself to get clients. There are tons of people out there who want to convince you their marketing process is the way to go and that's not to say it doesn't work. For example, I am a huge fan of repurposing content and having a system to do that.

If I record a podcast, I want to distribute that thing everywhere, get it transcribed, and use it on social media. Why? Because it's efficient and it makes my life easier. However, if you are someone who loathes recording an audio or creating a video, you are going to struggle with creating content in order to repurpose. The content is the catalyst to get people into your business ecosystem and the conversion tool you use to get them to go from prospect to client.

But before you can step into a repurposing system, or any sales or marketing system for that matter, you have actually discern *how* you are going to create that content in the first place because ultimately being a good marketer comes down to how you are connecting with your prospective clients, which boils down to content.

Which brings me to the throat center . . . the throat center is where all of the energy wants to come out of our bodies and into the world. The throat is where we give words, and ultimately voice, to the energy within. This is how we communicate with others and interact with the world around us. This is where we can discern how we can best communicate our gifts with the world as entrepreneurs.

Each gate coming off of the throat center will discern how best you communicate with the world when you are in congruence with your strategy and authority. There are eleven gates coming off of the throat center that will give life to our communication style. These are sometimes referred to as the voices of the throat center. The style in which you will communicate depends upon what is activated in your chart.

The healthy throat is a reliable source of communication. The throat can express or act from six different centers.

1. **The heart** (gate 45) speaks from the "I" or "I want that, I have that, I will do that"—take leadership.
2. **The ajna** (gate 62, gate 23, gate 56) speaks what the mind is thinking and conceptualizing—speak your mind.
3. **The solar plexus** (gate 12, gate 35) speaks or acts on the emotions or feelings—express your feelings.
4. **The spleen** (gate 16) speaks spontaneously, intuitively, and knowingly in the moment—speak your intuition.
5. **The sacral** (gate 20) speaks through the responsive sounds of the sacral in the moment—manifest your action through words.
6. **The identity** speaks from personal identity, self-expression, and direction from the higher self—make a unique creative contribution.

Understanding the energy you have in your throat will help you discern how to communicate. Once you understand that energy, you can then leverage your type, profile, and strategy and authority to discern how best to market yourself.

A channel will always have more potent, consistent energy than a gate. First, start by looking at the channels coming off of your throat, then you look at the gates.

I'll use myself as an example here. I have gate 62 which is known as the sense maker; I have gate 16 (which is also my incarnation cross), which is I experiment, also known as the master; and I have gate 12, which is I try, also known as the wordsmith. If you take a look at the content I post across my social media, you will see these themes sprinkled throughout.

Once you have a clear understanding of your channels and gates, you can then discern how best you can integrate your voice into your marketing.

If you have an undefined throat, know that you can oscillate between all of the gates, but the reliable energy will be in the gates you have defined.

With an open throat, you will be able to float between all of the different voices of the throat, so learning to rely on your strategy and authority will be key.

It is through this energy within the throat center that you can learn to reliably and consistently give voice to your marketing efforts.

Now the medium with which you do that will vary greatly depending upon your type and profile, which I will share tips on later in this section. However, I recommend experimenting, and part of the reason I recommend this is because I believe the different energies of the throat manifest in different ways. For example, I believe my gate 12 manifests itself in my writing, whereas my gates 62 and 16 tend to make themselves known via video and audio. You might find this to be true for you.

Where the gates and channel are coming from is also important; for example, gate 16 flows from the spleen and operates intuitively in the now, while channel 62-17 flows from the ajna and make sense of the world in the now, since they are both part of the knowing circuit. Whereas my gate 12 comes from the solar plexus, and 12 is rooted in the collective circuit and must be in the mood. I find this to be very true for me to be able to write. I must be in the mood to do so.

Before I get into the voices of the gates, I firmly believe that marketing in general should be based in story, and we can use the voices of the gates to bring that story to life via the medium of our choosing. But the story becomes the vehicle with which we share. In order to understand what stories and knowing are appropriate for you to share, let's look to the voices of the gates.

The Voices of the Gates

- Gate 62: I think—the left brain voice of reason—details are your superpower
- Gate 23: I know—the ability to articulate things in new ways—individual insights that shine a new light, and your voice will have a deep knowing
- Gate 56: I believe—the right brain power of telling stimulating stories at the right time

- Gate 16: I experiment—an enthusiasm and zest for life—an inclination to leap into new experiences and an uncanny capacity to wing it—passion drives mastery through repetition over time
- Gate 35: I feel—the ability to have many talents and share those experiences—value adventure and being alive
- Gate 20: I am—speaking in the present with an innate knowing of when to manifest power/action/clarity by inspiring others and connecting people and resources
- Gate 12: I try—speaking to the depth of humanity's highs and lows when in the mood—this has an oscillating bold/shy/in the mood nature
- Gate 31: I lead—being called into leadership by others at the right time, place, and call
- Gate 8: I can—transformation to support others in their creative contributions—unique self-expression
- Gate 33: I remember—the right brain ability to look back on the past and reflect on what has gone in order to improve the future
- Gate 45: I have—the teacher/leader speaking to guide the community with an individualistic flair for their own path—lead through teaching

Using the voice of the gates above can help you discern how best to actually give life to the energy inside of you and communicate that to the world via your marketing, then you discern the medium that is in congruence based on your unique Human Design blueprint.

A Note about Gates Reaching Toward the Throat Center

You might also find that you experience some of the energy of the gates that are reaching toward the throat center. For example, in my chart gate 11 and gate 10 are two gates that are reaching to the throat center. Since there is only one gate to bridge that energy, you may also find that energy present in your chart as well since we often embody the polarity of what is present in our chart. This is very nuanced, so I don't want you to spend hours hemming and hawing over it. I simply want to mention it in case you find yourself using the language of one of the other gates.

For me this might show up as me expressing my own individuality . . . or I believe this to be true based on my understanding. I only mention this not to confuse or add a layer of complexity but because I think you may see it appear in your own chart, and I believe it is important for you to understand where it comes from.

While you will not always have consistent access to this energy, it may be present for you because, remember, all of the energy in the chart wants to flow out of the body via the throat.

With gates, you are always magnetizing people to you as well as the opposite gate. For example, I am always magnetizing a gate 20 or 56 to me because they complete the flow. You might find this to be helpful in a coworking situation or with team members.

SALES

et's face it, sales is a dirty word . . . People *love* to buy, but they hate to be sold to. The goal for me with every client is to create ease when selling. When you can decrease resistance in the buying process, you will increase sales. When you decrease resistance, you increase flow. Sales doesn't have to be a dirty word, so let's reframe your relationship with sales.

For me, sales is simply the exchange of money for your services. It is an energetic exchange. At its most fundamental level, "you give me money, I give you information or this widget." It is the bargain or agreement made between two people. Over time, sales has gotten a bad name because of cold calling and sleazy tactics. I know I have gone to a car dealership and have told the person I am just looking simply because I didn't want to be bothered or sold to. No one likes to be talked at or pitched to.

We aren't here for any of those yucky tactics because we want to sell in congruence with our Human Design. When we sell in congruence with our design, we end up in flow, and it is a beautiful thing. Selling can be easy when we make buying simple for the prospective client.

This starts by creating marketing content. This marketing content will serve as the tool to get people into our business ecosystem, and ultimately, that same content will also drive them onto our sales page and/or to booking a call with us in order to have a buying conversation or purchasing online.

The reality is people buy from people they know, like, and trust. So the question then becomes how can I quickly build trust in a relationship with someone I haven't met via marketing and my sales page? Again, this comes down to story and becoming aware of what people's preconceived notions might be about you. This is also known as "thin-slicing" in Malcolm Gladwell's book *Blink*. The example he uses is about an art dealer who can't pinpoint what is wrong with the statue, but he knows it is a fake.

Thin-slicing is when people subconsciously make snap judgments about you based on their past lived experiences. It happens whether you like it or not, and that thin slice impacts your ability to sell. When I teach this in my Business Ecosystem Builders program, we spend four to five weeks on this, so don't feel pressure to get this all figured out. I simply want you to become aware of the fact that these thin slices are happening on social media, in your marketing, on your sales page, and on your discovery calls.

Your job becomes how do I combat those snap judgments in order to create flow in the buying process. We start by first understanding what those snap judgments are. This is a really challenging exercise if you know someone or have interacted with them, but it is important to discern what that initial judgment is.

For me, when I was in my twenties in business, I used to get "know it all," "preschool teacher," "lawyer," "young" (which often implies inexperienced) and more. I would then use story as a vehicle to reframe these snap judgments.

In my website design business, I'd often tell the story of how I coded my own *Frogger* game at twelve, or when I transitioned to coaching, I'd share the story of how I used to read textbooks and create my own exercises from them, teaching anyone who would listen (ah, my Projector self was so out of congruence). The reality is these stories were a vehicle I could use without sounding self-aggrandizing, while also reframing and building trust with clients.

I recommend grabbing a notebook and beginning to think about some stories that you could use in order to help reframe those initial impressions people might make of you. Begin using them in your sales conversations at the onset of the conversation, on your about page, and in your marketing efforts.

Now, of course, try to do all of this is while keeping in congruence with your strategy and authority. How this emerges will differ for each of us but understand that making the buying process easy and building trust are the bedrocks of the sales process.

The reality is though, you want to make it easy for people to buy from you, and you don't want to make people jump through a lot of different hoops in order to do so. Even if you can't make all your products and services available for purchase online, I recommend making some of them available online for ease of purchase and getting into your business ecosystem.

SALES & MARKETING
FOR PROJECTORS

For Projectors to be in success, which is their signature theme, they need to allow themselves to be seen. This is not always the easiest task for Projectors since many of them may hold bitterness and resentment because they have often offered up advice without an invitation.

The reality is that a big part of the Projector's role is to show up online in congruence with their purpose and their depth of wisdom. This means offering up wisdom via the form of social media, sharing what you are passionate about and working on while "resting" and sharing your unique self along the way.

Of course, the medium (podcast, text, etc.) will vary from Projector to Projector; the important thing is that allowing yourself to be seen and exploring the depths of your wisdom publicly will ensure you receive recognition and invitations along the way.

With respect to the sales process, it is important for the Projector to wait for the recognition or sale before pitching someone. It would be better for a Projector to avoid sending out cold, unsolicited messages or pitching someone a program, instead of waiting for the other person to ask, "How can I work with you?" Waiting for the sense of energetic congruence will ensure the Projector doesn't end up selling to someone who hasn't recognized the Projector for their amazing wisdom and doesn't end up in a situation where they feel bitter and resentful.

When a Projector is in congruence, they will usually feel a sense of ease and flow. Recognition and invitations won't stop flowing when the Projector is in their power. They will share their offerings via their marketing efforts, and people will almost magically appear. People will be constantly asking, "How can I buy from you?"

It is important for Projectors to be mindful of not saying yes to every invitation that comes along if it doesn't feel like a yes for them. Projectors will often settle for the next invitation that comes along because they feel like they have been waiting for so long. This is not correct for them. It's a good idea for Projectors to only accept invitations that feel good to them, otherwise the energy to follow through won't be there for them.

Projectors with emotional authority who need to ride their wave before entering a contract with a new client or a bigger deal will often find themselves being hounded by others simply because they seem elusive and "hard to get" when in reality they are simply giving themselves the space to discern whether this is right for them.

SALES & MARKETING
FOR GENERATORS

For Generators to be in congruence with their signature theme of satisfaction with respect to their marketing and sales, they must be responding. Responding in the marketing world could mean asking communities, "What kind of content do you want from me?"

For example, "I am a copywriting coach who helps female copywriters charge $20K a sales page; what kind of content would you want me to share?"

When a Generator asks a question like this, this gives them something to respond to based on all the questions that they will get in the comments. This is a great way for a Generator to come up with content topics for whatever medium they plan to use.

For Generators, using their content to create more to respond to keeps them in their dance with the world because a healthy Generator is constantly dancing with the universe as it gives things to respond to.

Engagement and calls to action will suit the Generator well as keep them in the dance with life. This helps them build relationships with their community as well, which is incredibly important to the Generator.

In terms of which medium is best for a Generator, look at the throat and then tap into the sacral response to discern which way to create content. Do I want to do video? Do I want to do a podcast? Do I want to write a blog post?

In the sales process, the Generator will likely want to wait for the other to ask about their offerings before going into the pitching process. Inviting the other person into a dialogue will keep the Generator in that dance of response while also feeling that energetic pull if the person is correct for them to work with.

As a Generator, when you are working with someone new, you may feel yourself light up from the inside. It often feels exciting, and you may feel a pull to work with them. If this doesn't happen, they might not be the correct person for you.

SALES & MARKETING
FOR MANIFESTORS

Manifestors are here to initiate and inform, and that is exactly what you can do on social media to live in congruence with your design. Now, for Manifestors, the traditional marketing wisdom of showing up consistently is not going to work for them. You will need to show up when you have the energy to support those initiations.

Use your marketing efforts as a way to inform others of what you are doing, what you are working on, and your plans along the way. Marketing is a great way to keep your community informed of your business. Of course, you will need to discern which medium you will use based on your throat activations.

With respect to selling, this can be a challenge for the Manifestor because they like to initiate, so building a sales strategy where you reach out *may* feel like you are in congruence with your design simply because that is how you are designed to operate, but obviously lean into it if that feels correct for you as that will not be correct for all Manifestors.

On the sales call, you will want to lead and that's appropriate for you. Your work is potent and catalytic in nature. You often like to get in, get people a transformation, and get out, so discerning who is right for the transformative nature of your work is important. Other people will respond to you, so don't be afraid to tell it like it is and be direct with people. Inform them of how your work will render them better off in the sales call or on the conversion tool like a sales page.

As a Manifestor, you can be bold in your sales and marketing. This polarizing way will draw the correct people to you, and you will transform their world and then go back to refueling your energy until your next initiation arrives.

SALES & MARKETING FOR MANIFESTING GENERATORS

Marketing and sales for Manifesting Generators is a thing of beauty. I have witnessed MGs effortlessly marketing their business through embodying their uniqueness, focusing on their own garden, and showing up with ease.

Now if you are an MG, you might be thinking, "Marketing is a challenge for me . . ." and it might be, but know that to the outside world, you appear effortless. You stand tall, showing others what it means to be themselves and empowering others to do the same simply by sharing your story and gifts.

To the MG, putting themselves out into the world maybe a challenge. Many MGs want to ensure they know enough before they share so they are able to back up their stance. This often leads them to avoid marketing until they feel ready; however, this often doesn't stop the MG from growing their business as they often have multiple irons in the fire due to their multipassionate ways and the many relationships they seamlessly juggle.

Many MGs I've worked with over the years have taken a minimalist approach to marketing yet somehow against all odds have grown their businesses. I have found this to be true because they have built relationships where they can leverage the different parts of themselves and grow via those relationships.

An MG's strategy is to visualize the outcome, respond, and inform—this is how they can show up in their marketing efforts. MGs will often do well when they have someone to bounce ideas off of and support them in the implementation of the marketing. Since MGs move quickly, they will often skip steps, and having someone with a high attention to detail to help them will be beneficial to them in their marketing.

In terms of sales, I recommend every MG put up a waitlist before they launch anything. This will gauge interest to see whether what they are doing is worth the energy/effort. This gives them something to respond to, and then the MG can inform people of what's happening when the time is correct for them.

SALES & MARKETING FOR REFLECTORS

For Reflectors, their environment determines their success. If the environment is wrong, they will struggle to find success in their marketing and sales. Since Reflectors are nonenergy beings, they won't want to be juggling multiple marketing efforts or platforms. Same goes for sales. They will want to focus and cultivate on one platform and build a community that feels really good to them and that's a mirror of the world they are creating.

For you as a Reflector, having a very supportive work environment is important. This means you will likely want to have a set place to work and a set community space for your marketing efforts. You are a mirror of those you are around, so it is key for you to discern the tone you want to set for your marketing efforts and sales conversations.

If you are feeling off, you likely need to cultivate your community. You have deep wisdom about humankind, and you can leverage that wisdom to create content, share stories, and showcase the depth of humanity. You are a deep person with a great deal of knowledge about the world since you are so open. This is a great gift when it comes to sales and marketing. However, in the wrong communities, you will feel the toxicity, and it won't feel good to you.

You will be welcomed in by those around you when you have gotten the environment and community correct, and your efforts with sales and marketing will give you a sense of happiness. When launching something new, you will often need to give yourself lots of space to discern whether a marketing effort or sales offer is correct. Take the time and space you need to get it correct. This space and time will give you the insights you need in order to move forward. This space will make sure you end up in the correct environment at the correct time with the correct people.

SALES & MARKETING
FOR FIRST LINES

For first lines, it is important to establish a solid foundation in order for you to feel confident in your marketing and sales. This means you will need to give yourself a set period of time where you allow yourself to do the research on how you will market yourself, and then you will need to move into action. This could mean taking baby steps, but you will need to begin by putting one foot in front of another as a first line can find themselves researching forever. It is through the consistent repetition of leveraging one medium over and over again that a first line will gain confidence.

Trying new platforms or mediums will be uncomfortable for the first lines, and they will feel a deep need to know all the pieces. Set yourself up with a time-frame during which you will allow yourself to do the research before moving forward, or hire an expert to help support you in taking on a new medium.

In sales, a first line is going to want to have a clearly laid out plan with all the details and nuances and pitfalls that may come up along the way. They want to create clear products to whom they can sell.

Selling can feel uncomfortable to them as they tend to be on the introverted side, and they get nervous that they will not necessarily know all the answers to the questions that someone might seek. If you are playing in your zone of genius, you must learn to trust that you have done the work to establish yourself as an expert. You are an expert even though the not-self of your mind might lead you to believe otherwise. You are a master of your craft, and the more repetition you have with respect to selling and marketing, the more confidence you will feel.

You are an expert, and you have put in the time to position yourself in that way. Your role in the sales call is to share your expertise without giving all of your knowledge away for free. You deserve to be paid well for your expertise, and balancing that on the sales call is key for you.

SALES & MARKETING
FOR SECOND LINES

M arketing and sales can be a challenge for the second line. You enjoy your alone time and do not enjoy coming out of your bubble and into the world. Your home is your safe space, so showing up to market may be a struggle.

I have found many second lines do well with posting and ghosting, meaning they post something on social media and then immediately get off of the platform. Again, the medium will differ based on your preference. but due to the nature of second lines, they typically do well with audio or written since they don't always want their face attached to everything.

In marketing, honor your pull to get in and then get out. Show up, do your thing, and then go back into your zone. This will honor your energy needs while simultaneously giving others something to call you out on and allowing them to recognize your gifts. Remember, second lines need someone to recognize their innate talents and gifts as they aren't always aware of them (or rather need others to help point those gifts out).

Inside the sales call, a second line will use their natural ability to get others talking and will listen to/absorb the information they receive. It is imperative that they actually ask for the sale to solidify the relationship and move the person from prospect to client.

Sales systems like a sales page or things that ease the buying process are helpful to the second line. Making it easy for all of your products to be purchased online and only having minimal sales conversations is definitely going to have the most ease for the second line. You will need to package and price your services accordingly and outline all the details of what is included if you opt to go this route.

I would also recommend if you plan to avoid doing discovery calls that you have lots of testimonials on your site and give an option for people who have questions to reach out to you via email, chat widget, or Voxer.

SALES & MARKETING
FOR THIRD LINES

As a third line, experimenting with your marketing and sales is key. Innovate, create, play, and have fun. Try new things. Dive in and know you will figure it out along the way, and if not, you will at least learn something new. Marketing for you is a playground with which you can experiment to see what works for you and your audience.

Now, you may have felt like you've tried and failed, and therefore, you are afraid to try again. Remember, as a third line, you are not your failures. You simply move through the world by learning and trying. You get to enjoy the variety of life and taste what you like and what you don't. You get to use these experiences to share your lessons with others on how not to do things.

In your marketing, this translates to being discerning about what you like to do and how you like to do it. It means trying new things and dropping them when they don't work for you. It means not being afraid to do something in your own way.

In sales, the same applies, so perhaps you take the nontraditional route for sales calls. Perhaps you offer Voxer access for the sales calls, or you have them reach out via chat. Experiment away and think outside the box about what works for you.

As a third line, because of your trial-and-error experimentation process, you bring a depth of wisdom to any conversation you enter. You may take this information for granted as this is how you experience the world; *however*, this experience allows you to help others shortcut things. Don't give all this information away for free; don't take it for granted. It is invaluable to help others move forward faster, so share some of it on a sales call, but not all of it.

As a third line, you also have a gift for seeing what won't work out faster than others, and this applies to marketing, people, software, and well, just about everything. This can be both a blessing and a curse in sales and marketing.

Learning to balance your urge to break bonds while also honoring the fact that not everyone will move as quickly as you do in the sales and marketing process is important. Breathe, pause, and give others space to make decisions on their time before breaking the bond.

SALES & MARKETING
FOR FOURTH LINES

A fourth line's success is in direct correlation to the quality of their network. Building a quality network is critical for fourth lines. This doesn't necessarily mean you need to know people in person in a traditional networking way, by any means. It simply means that building a community and a network of people is going to help you grow your business with more ease.

This means as a best practice, you will want to show up consistently online in a way that is in congruence with your design and build quality relationships. For you, it isn't about quantity; it is about quality. The more quality relationships you can build to pull people into your world, the faster you will be able to grow.

As a fourth line, your people come to you through the people already inside of your network. For example, you have someone in your program and they tell a friend about it. This is how you grow. Knowing this is the key to your success as it allows you to build relationships—this might mean that creating and establishing an affiliate relationship or a referral program might be of great benefit to you. This incentivizes people to support you while also working to your strengths.

Creating opportunities where you can speak in front of other people's groups, be a guest on podcasts, and anything where you can leverage someone else's audience will be a great strategy for you as it is directly in congruence with the fourth line way of growing your network.

In terms of sales calls, you will do best with people who know you through someone else. Your messaging often won't resonate with someone who has never met you before. That's not to say that it won't work. It may, but it simply isn't typical even if everything looks good on paper. A deal with someone who is a cold contact will often fall apart for the fourth line.

SALES & MARKETING
FOR FIFTH LINES

As a fifth line, you live and breathe in the projection field, meaning people may have expectations of you that you aren't willing to fulfill. Fifth lines are often called in to save the day when all other traditional routes have failed and people need to try a new way of doing things.

As a fifth line, it is incredibly important to be clear and consistent in your messaging. It is even more important to be direct in your sales conversation about what you are willing to do (and what you are not willing to do). Solid contracts are a fifth line's best friend, simply because they live in the projection field. Oftentimes, they may say things over and over again, but people may not actually hear what they have to say simply because they have an expectation in their mind of what they believe the fifth line can do for them.

Fifth lines will need to discern the medium that works best for them to offer up their storytelling marketing. They may even want to oscillate between different mediums in order to allow others to hear that consistent message in different ways and really be clear on what they, the fifth line, are willing to support people with. Showing up may be a challenge for a fifth line, and they will need to get clear on what they are willing to share on social media and in their marketing as they tend to be private and very deep people. Most people will not see the full depth of the fifth line, so the fifth line must get clear on what pieces of themselves they want to be seen in the online world.

I bring this up as the voice of experience; the fifth line projection field is quite wild. It simply amazes me how clear I can be, yet inevitably certain people who have a different expectation of me will hear something completely different. However, I have found that as I have become more clear in my message, have been more grounded in my being, and have been living more in congruence with myself, the disconnect of the projection field has greatly lessened. So if you are a fifth line, and you are experiencing lots of turbulence, you may be out of congruence with your purpose and the work you are here to do.

In sales, it's a good idea for fifth lines to let the other talk, which will come naturally to the private fifth line. This will allow the fifth line to decide whether they would like to come in and save the day or not. If they are willing to support this person or not. If they can meet the expectations of the person or not. Or if they need to create clarity in the relationship.

A tip I've heard for fifth lines that they can use to break up the projection field is to wear a hat or a bright piece of clothing since it breaks up the energy. Ra Uru Hu, the founder of Human Design, was a fifth line and always wore a hat. For me personally, I always wear hats simply because it makes me feel good and it feels like it keeps my energy intact, especially in group settings. You might want to try this and see whether it works for you as a fifth line.

SALES & MARKETING
FOR SIXTH LINES

Since sixth lines have three phases, it is important for you to discern which phase you are in to determine what is best for you during that phase. If you are in the first phase of the sixth line, you can take the strategies of the third line and apply them.

During the second phase, you will likely be establishing yourself and setting a foundation for success during your third phase. This means you can incorporate some of the strategies discussed in the second line section since the second phase of the sixth line is a very inward phase. It is a phase of discovery and laying the foundation for what comes in the third phase.

During the third phase of the sixth line, when the sixth line gets their wings, they will often be able to grow their business with ease through referral. Many sixth lines who have laid a solid foundation in phase two will be able to show up in their marketing periodically, and their business will often grow by referral sort of behind the scenes without a lot of effort on their part.

Since during phase three the sixth line is embodying what it means to be the most authentic version of themselves, they can simply exist, doing their thing, and they will magnetize work to them almost like magic. I have two clients with a sixth line in their profile, and they have a very sporadic online presence, but their business is booming because they laid the foundation during the second phase of their sixth line.

As a sixth line, simply being yourself in sales and marketing will bring the right people into your world while honoring your strategy and authority. While you may want to actively market yourself, many sixth lines find that podcasting or creating videos is a great way to connect with their audience. Writing a book as well is another great strategy for a sixth line since they can share the depth of their wisdom, and this will serve as a marketing tool to attract clients again and again.

A VERY IMPORTANT NOTE ON EMOTIONAL AUTHORITY...

I f you have emotional authority or you are dealing with people with emotional authority, clarity does not come in the now. Clarity comes over time, and ultimately, you will never have 100 percent buy-in from yourself or from the other. I mention this here because I see so many people especially Manifestors, Generators, and Manifesting Generators who get themselves into situations of the not-self because they didn't honor their emotional authority and get to an emotional neutral before making a decision.

When you have emotional authority, you need time. Clarity comes over the passing of time. This could mean a day or two or a week, but I promise you clarity will come. This clarity might mean a 70 or 80 percent knowing of what is correct for you. You will never have 100 percent buy-in *yes* or buy-out *no*. If you do have 70 or 80 percent, that is what is correct for you. You can say yes or no, trusting you are making the correct decision. Honor this. Otherwise you will spend a lifetime in a holding pattern, not making any decisions or taking years to make a decision and opportunities will pass you by. I say this from experience.

Conversely, with the buying process, it is also important to honor those with emotional authority, especially if you are not an emotional authority. People with emotional authority need time and space to discern whether something is correct for them. Their knowing does not come in the now. Offer them a time frame with which to make these decisions so that you don't end up with a client who regrets working with you.

A VERY IMPORTANT NOTE FOR THOSE WITH A DEFINED HEART...

For those of you with a defined heart (also known as the will center), it is important to be aware that you can impose your will on those in your presence. Over 60 percent of the population has an undefined will center. With a defined will center, those in your presence with an undefined will center can borrow your willpower, and you can convince them that anything is possible.

I have found it crucial inside of the sales conversation to open a dialogue around what they believe is possible for them vs. "telling" them what you believe is possible. Ask questions, be genuinely curious, and dig deeper—words like "meaning," "how so," "because," and "tell me more" will help you glean insight into the true desires of an undefined will center.

While your defined heart can be a gift, and it can help you to have the willpower to follow through, commit, and move forward quickly—this same willpower can also "convince people" inside of a sales conversation that something is for them when it is not, and the same goes for your marketing efforts.

You are the ultimate *hype* person when you have a defined will center, and this can work to your advantage in coaching; however, you do not want it to interfere with the buying and decision-making processes.

I find that giving people the gift of time and space to allow that borrowed willpower to wear off before they make a buying decision to be helpful so that you don't end up in a situation where someone said yes and then becomes a headache because they made a decision from the not-self of the undefined heart or out of congruence with their authority.

PRODUCTIVITY

When I think about productivity, I can't help but think about the toxic culture we have here in the United States with hustle culture. Many of us tie our productivity to our worth.

I distinctly remember how much time I've had to spend unwinding the idea that if it is between 9 a.m. and 5 p.m., I "should be working," but the reality is I am most productive in the morning between 4 a.m. and 7 a.m. My creativity soars at that point, and maybe it is because of all the distractions during the day or maybe it is just how I am designed. I often can get more done in those three hours than most can get done in a day.

The reality is our "productivity" is not tied to what we accomplish or do. We are already worthy simply by existing. The not-self of this hustle culture is often tied to the pressure center of the root—the source of all stress in the body a.k.a. the pressure/urgency to do—and the motor center of the sacral—the source of all doing in the body.

When it comes to productivity, I firmly believe we each have a code to unlock when it comes to what works for us. Some of you may need to be in the mood to get work done, while others can simply get up and do. Discerning what works for you and at what time of day will help you get clear on your productivity style.

The not-self of the mind will try to trick you when it comes to productivity, and getting to know that not-self is a big part of getting into congruence and allowing ease into your life. Again, congruence is going to be different from person to person based on your past lived experiences, your story, your strategy and authority, and your goals when it comes to creating the life you desire.

Before I get into understanding the gates of the sacral, I want to encourage you to throw out everything you think "you know" about productivity. Throw out all the tips and tricks shared from the many productivity experts and time management experts. I encourage you to let go of the things that you are supposed to do, and instead act in congruence with some values that work for you when it comes to productivity.

As we go through this section, I want to remind you that the world we are living in is designed to keep you occupied, distracted, and unfocused—the ever present ding of a text or a notification, a reminder from an app to meditate, and the seemingly endless bombardment of demands on your time from the devices we surround ourselves with. These notifications mean well in theory, under the guise of "never miss a notification (FOMO) or keep you on track with your habits and therefore keeping you healthy." While I believe there is a time and a place for these amazing tools, they can also run our lives seemingly without our awareness. These devices, apps, and programs are designed to keep us distracted, demand our attention, and keep us connected to them, instead of us being intentional with our time.

For me, the goal is to be in-distractable. Do I leverage these tools? Yes. But do I do it on my terms, not theirs? Yes.

When you think about your productivity, you have to take into account everything we've been talking about in this course thus far and what the lifestyle you want to create is like. What do you want your life to look like? If your goal is to build a multimillion-dollar business, your "productivity" is going to be very different than if you were to build a $250K business. Before I dig into the productivity aspect, I want you to anchor yourself in what *you* want your life to look like. How much do you actually want to work?

Work will expand into time allowed. This is a slippery slope, especially for entrepreneurs like you and me who work from home. The boundaries between working hours and at home time can blur, making it incredibly difficult to get clear on "what you are doing." For example, if I take my laptop downstairs to write an email in the living room while my kids are playing Nintendo, that email will likely take me two hours to write. This is in part because there are lots of interruptions and distractions, in part because I'm trying to write later in the day when it is hard for me to get into the writing zone, and in part because I firmly believe that if you have two hours to get something done, it will fill up those two hours.

When allocating time to get things done, I believe most entrepreneurs struggle with one thing or a combination of three things.

1. The task is too big for the time allotted.
2. The task is too small for the time allotted.
3. There is no set task for the time I have allotted to get things done.

I'll use the example of a sales page. Many entrepreneurs will block time to get a sales page done, but they don't specify what part of that sales page they will work on during that time. Instead of going in and working on graphics or copy or something specific, they go in and just "work," not really being productive. Working on the sales page was too big of a task to get done in one hour.

Conversely, I've seen many entrepreneurs who are like, "I gave myself an hour to write a social media post." While certainly some social media posts may take an hour to write, the vast majority take way less. Therefore, they allotted *too* much time for the task at hand.

I've also witnessed many entrepreneurs claim that "it's going to take me forever to get through this email." Then when asked how long is it going to take, they say sixty focused minutes.

Many entrepreneurs, myself included, want to "work on our businesses." So we block the time to do the work, yet we neglect to discern what we will do during that time. So the time comes and we think to ourselves, *Let me just hop on and check Facebook or Instagram or TikTok real quick, then I will get to work.* An hour or two passes by and we are like, "Oh sh*t, I must go do x now," and we missed the opportunity to be productive when it would have benefited us the most.

You are not alone in this. I have experienced this myself and witnessed client after client struggle with these same things. The reality is our time here is precious. Our time is our most valuable asset. Our time is not renewable. We don't get a second chance at any hour or day.

A dear friend of mine said, "I am a snob about my time." And that has really stuck with me because when we can be more intentional with our time, we can more intentionally create our lives.

For many of us, we need focused, distraction (and notification) free time in order to reach our potential. This happens when we can clearly outline our days and weeks, set goals, and follow the ebbs and flows of energy while crossing things off of our to-do list.

I truly believe it is not about the number of hours you work; it is about the potency of that hour. It is about the value you bring to the tasks you accomplish in that hour. It is about what you can accomplish when you bring intention to your work instead of allowing the demands on your attention to run your day. You run your day, not your phone, or your app, or your social media, or your clients. *You.*

Of course, this brings up the conundrum of what I can do in an hour, you might not be able to do and vice versus. It again becomes about knowing who you are, understanding what your strengths are, and leveraging your talents while getting support for the areas you may struggle with. Understanding this is often the key that unlocks the next level for many of my clients. If you have never done a time study, I highly recommend you do one. It's uncomfortable, and it brings a level of awareness that you'd otherwise would never have.

I do a time study once a quarter. A time study involves writing down what you are doing every fifteen minutes for two weeks and labeling it—Strategic, Tactical, Self-Care, and Personal/Family/Friend time. While you don't have to do this, it provides great insight into where and how you are spending your time so you can bring more intention to your time. I will tell you from firsthand experience, it is uncomfortable, it is eye-opening, and you probably aren't using your time as wisely as you thought. So buckle up. Please note this is *not* required; it is simply an exercise you can use to bring awareness to your time. I will often have clients do this activity when they are trying to figure out who to hire on their team next or which activities they can delegate, so you might find that useful as well.

PRODUCTIVITY AND THE SACRAL CENTER

First, let's start by understanding where the gates are headed within the Human Design chart. This will give us an understanding of the themes that you will experience within the gates.

Gates connect to the

- Identity Center—These gates are focused on direction and authentic connection.
- Throat Center—These gates are about empowering your voice.
- Spleen Center—These gates are focused on securing your safety and nourishment.
- Root Center—This energy is known as format energy and has an influence over the entire chart. The gates connected to the root center are the pressure to do or bring something to fruition.
- Solar Plexus—These gates provide the energy to create and bond (develop intimacy).

Now let's dive into the meanings behind the gates.

Gates Connected to the Identity Center
- Gate 5—Create patterns or rhythms for the flow of your energy.

- Gate 14—Generate energy for the creation of resources, especially for others.
- Gate 29—Generate perseverance (and surrender) to anything you say "yes" to.
- Gate 34—Your energy empowers your authentic action.

Gates Connected to the Solar Plexus

- Gate 59—This gate provides the energy to create or bond both with a partner or in business (this energy flows to the will center).

Gates Connected to the Root

Format energy—This activates the root energy into action or not and influences the entire chart.

- Gate 9—The energy to focus and concentrate. Remember all gates and channels hold duality or dichotomy, so the opposite may also be true, and many people with this gate or the whole channel may be diagnosed with ADHD.
- Gate 3—The mutative energy to start something new, bring order to from chaos, to bring something new form.
- Gate 42—The energy of entering into cycles and finishing them. Completing what has been started. You may struggle to get into action with this gate, but once in action, you complete cycles.

Gates Connected to the Spleen

- Gate 27—This energy is strong, tribal, protective, and nourishing energy.
- Gate 34—You will use your energy to empower your survival.

Gates Connected to the Throat

- Gate 34—You will use your energy to empower your voice.

Understanding Your Productive Energy

Understanding the energy you have within the sacral will help you understand how best to be productive. It will give discernment to the energy you have when in the doing, which is ultimately the basis of being productive. You will also be able to recognize when the doing energy is not your own, and you can shift your state so that you are in the doing of your zone of genius.

I have the format energy of gate 9, and as a non-sacral being, I can often and easily get stuck in the on position "doing." Focusing for hours at a time. This can also erupt as complete squirrel syndrome where I am jumping from task to task, not getting anything done. This is a flag to me that I need to walk away from the task at hand.

A Note for Sacral Beings

If you are a sacral being—Generators and Manifesting Generators—you will have a full channel (or multiple channels) and a defined sacral. This will be energy that is always present and your default for doing. Then your gate energy will take precedence. You will have the ability to do and get things done.

Most Generators don't like to be interrupted and will often struggle to get back on task once they have been nudged or distracted. The key for the Generator is to give yourself focused time for your methodical ways. Generators aren't meant to switch gears from task to task; they are meant to stay focused on one task at hand.

Most Manifesting Generators will want to bounce from task to task and will be able to switch gears seamlessly and easily; in fact, that process will work best for them. Manifesting Generators *can* be multitaskers. It's OK for them to be juggling multiple balls in the air. It's OK for them to be bouncing from task to task. Yes, they may skip steps along the way, but this is part of their process. They will need to go back or hire someone to support them.

A Note for Non-Sacral Beings

If you are a non-sacral being—Projector, Manifestor, Reflector—you will be able to discern what energy is yours by understanding your gates, as in the example above with my gate 9 energy of focusing. Understanding which energy is yours will help you figure out whether you are pushing your body beyond its limits.

This is very common with nonenergy beings since they are being conditioned by energy beings. Learning to discern which energy is yours and listening to your body's cues about when it is time to stop is incredibly important for non-sacral beings so that they don't face burnout.

For Projectors, you are not here to do, you are here to guide; however, I am a reasonable person and I realize that for many Projectors, it is not realistic for you to do nothing. I know this is true for me in my business. Honoring the ebbs and flows of your energy is important and recognizing when you are stuck in the on position is incredibly important (as well as learning your body's cues). When I first learned about my Projector ways, I opted to give myself short time blocks to work so that I could learn to recognize my body's cues.

For Manifestors, your energy is going to come in bursts where you will be able to work for a few days at a time, and then you will need to rest. You have great starting power, but you may struggle to finish things. Know this about yourself so that you can go back and finish or get support with finishing.

For Reflectors, honoring the right environment to do the work will be key to your success. Make sure you have a space where you feel good about working and doing, and the energy will follow.

OFFERS & SYSTEMS

I firmly believe that when it comes to offers and systems, the advice traditionally handed out is to launch one thing and then another and then another but never actually learning, implementing, and improving on that which we have already done.

I believe in the concept of focusing and following one course until successful, especially when it comes to offers. Now, that doesn't mean that we won't tweak or adjust the offer along the way; in fact, I encourage it. However, that does mean we will give each idea and offer its due time to come to life in a way that is in congruence with our vision for it. It means we won't cast it aside if at first it isn't as successful as we had hoped.

It means we will nurture the offer so that it can become regenerative for us. So that it grows without our constant supervision. Creating a solid offer takes time and effort. We talked earlier about containers, which is the how of the delivery method of the offering you have. The offer is how you package it up and present it to the prospective clients.

I often find that people want to rush the process in order to get it over with, and then they end up with something that they are unhappy with. When you think about creating the ultimate offer, especially for your signature program or programs, you want it to be the ultimate value proposition. You want it to be priced at just the right amount of money (average money) and above-average value for that money. Finding that balance and sweet spot for your audience will take time on your part, but it's worth the effort in the long run.

For most businesses, you want to create an offer suite where you can usher a client along from one experience to the next as they grow and evolve on their journey. I think most entrepreneurs and business owners over time do this to some extent, or at the very minimum, they create referral relationships to offer people to the next step in their journey.

However, the *giant caveat* here is that people often "try" to do all of this at one time. Or over the course of a year. It has taken me nearly four years to create my offer suite and systematize it.

I bring this up because the last thing I want you to do is to try to get four different offers and systems implemented and then wonder why nothing is working and why you are burned out and overwhelmed.

I want to challenge you to focus on one signature offering over the course of a year and systematize it, streamline it, improve it, and nurture it, and ultimately build an ecosystem around it so it thrives.

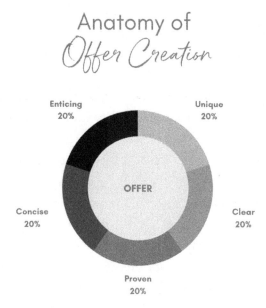

When I think about what goes into an offer, for me there are five different aspects to consider.

1. Unique—Is it unique and in congruence with who I am?
2. Clear—Could it easily be explained to a child?
3. Proven—Have I gotten results with clients before?
4. Concise—Am I delivering the information in a meaningful yet impactful way?
5. Enticing—Am I delivering above-average value for average pricing that the market will bear?

If you want to learn more about creating offers by design, I invite you to consider Business Design With Human Design—The Course.

Systems

When I talk to clients about systems in their business, I often get pushback: "Oh, systems don't work for me," or "I struggle to stick with it," or "I don't have a big enough team to implement systems."

I am here to let you in on a little secret . . . systems help you grow. They allow you to scale your business. They allow you to create an ecosystem for your offerings that create a better client experience, usher clients in a consistent way, and when done properly also bring in new clients repeatedly.

The Five Systems Every Business Needs

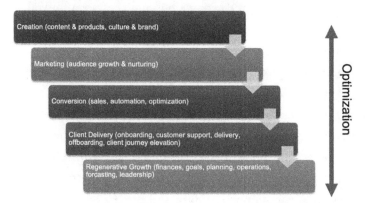

The reality is most entrepreneurs never make it through finishing and subsequently improving all of the different systems a business needs to thrive. Of course, it is in part due to glittery object syndrome, and many online coaches want to keep their clients in the hamster wheel in a cycle of launching and creating something new vs. optimizing and building a regenerative ecosystem. Also, it is human nature to want to create something new rather than spend time finishing something.

Unfortunately, I do not have a magic bullet when it comes to systems & offers and Human Design type & profile. From my experience, it is an iterative, coauthoring process that happens once you get clear on who you are, the lifestyle you want to create, and the business goals you have.

I will tell you from experience that it takes time; it takes about one year to get everything optimized and nurtured and get all of the systems in place. You can certainly do it in less time with a team, and for many of us, especially the non-sacral beings, we will need support in the implementation of these systems.

One thing, I'd like to note is that not all implementation is created equal. It is always more expensive to hire someone who is learning alongside you. I hired a team to help me with my *OMG Show* podcast about four years ago, and they told me they were optimizing and SEOing the blog. Turns out they were using words like "decision-making" to optimize my post. The problem is decision-making is searched millions of times a day and is an incredibly competitive search term. I can't tell you how many posts were "optimized" in this way. All of the work, time, money, effort, and energy for a very minimal return. Lesson learned, in true third line fashion.

Please take it from me that not all implementation is created equal, and as you go through the process of creating a business ecosystem for your offers and leveraging systems, implementation is what will make the difference between success and failure or between regenerative growth and nonregenerative growth that constantly needs your work, especially when it comes to systems like SEO, sales funnels, and client delivery.

I bring this up because hiring and delegating are hard for entrepreneurs like you and me. We struggle to give things to others because we often have the belief we can do it better ourselves—maybe that is true and maybe it is not.

Systems will set you free, but you have to start by creating them. A system could be a video of you simply recording your activity on how you do a certain task and speaking out loud how and why you are doing the things you do. I still have many videos I leverage from my social media agency days when I bring on a new support member to help me with something.

A system doesn't have to be a fancy Trello board, some planning app, or an intense spreadsheet. You can create a system simply by writing down the steps you take in a Word document. That is a system.

Now, systems can also be more complicated than that. They can include the use of tools, and in fact, as you grow, you might need to use tools to collaborate with your team. It's important for the tools to be selected based on the strengths and productivity style of the owner or entrepreneur, otherwise they will never use them. I know because this was me.

I'd also like to note that you don't need every piece or aspect of every system to get started. I am a big believer in starting small and layering things on top as you grow when it comes to systems.

For example, you don't need to have a whole content production system in place if it is just you and an assistant. You can layer that on over time.

Another example would be a conversion system. You can build a sales page first and then improve upon it over time. Same goes for client experience systems . . .

The goal isn't to get you to build all the pieces before you take action. The goal is to get you to build one piece, take action, build another, go through all five aspects of the systems, and then start again and build another layer on the same system.

For every client embarking on this journey of creating an offer, I almost always recommend doing a beta round or a founding member round to work out the kinks of any new offering.

A Note for *all* Beings

When discerning what offer to create, it is important to keep in mind what you want your weeks to look like. If you aren't clear about what you want, then any offer and container will get you to where you want to be. When you are clear about what you want, how many hours you want to work, and the level of involvement you will have with your clients, you can more easily discern what offer and container will work best for you. You can go back to the section on containers and go through the pitfalls of each.

With respect to creating systems in your business, I highly recommend you look at the channels and circuits present in your chart. If you have more of the logical circuitry, you will likely want to leverage tools that present in a more logical way. Conversely, if you have a lot of the sensing/visual circuitry, you will want to leverage tools that are more visual. That said, I am a huge fan of tools like MeisterTask where each person can adjust the view based on what suits them—visual or logical.

When selecting tools and systems, it's important for *you*, the business owner and entrepreneur, to be the one to discern which tools and systems your team uses, especially those that *you* will have to work within.

A Note for Sacral Beings

If you are a sacral being—Generators and Manifesting Generators—settling on an offer may be a challenge for you. The doing aspect of the offer creation process and systems will, for the most part, be easy for you, especially if and when you commit to the correct systems that support your style.

Most Generators will thrive at this deep work, but remember, Generators are here to do work they love . . . The key for the Generator is to give yourself focused time to go deep. Generators do not do well when they must switch gears from task to task or system to system. For them, picking something they love and sticking with it will be key.

While most Manifesting Generators will struggle to focus on just one offer and commit to just one system, understanding that they will need to juggle multiple things is important for them to *focus*. A great way for MGs to leverage these multitasking ways is to work on multiple things at once. This satisfies their urges and passions while also moving multiple things forward.

A Note for Non-Sacral Beings

If you are a non-sacral being—Projector, Manifestor, Reflector—you will have to manage the waxes and wanes of your energy in order to create an offer and the systems supporting it.

For Projectors, you are not here to do, you are here to guide, so creating offers and systems that require minimal amounts of your potent energy is key. Of course, I am a realist and know that many of us Projectors will need to be in the doing; however, it is important to keep our business systems minimalist, especially the ones we have to partake in.

For Manifestors, your energy is going to come in bursts where you will be able to work for a few days at a time and then you will need to rest. You have great starting power, but you may struggle to finish things. When it comes to creating new offers, this will be a strength of yours; however, many Manifestors will struggle to create systems since they are detail-oriented in nature, and the Manifestor will feel like it will slow them down—even though the converse is true.

For Reflectors, honoring the right environment to do the work will be the key to your success. Make sure you have a space where you feel good about working and doing, and the energy will follow.

WRAPPING UP THE HD YOUR BIZ BOOK—THE CONCLUSION

My hope is that at this point in the journey you have a better understanding of your Human Design and how to leverage that in your life and business. The journey to living in congruence with your Human Design takes time and grace. You must learn to dance with your design, tend to the aspects where you have gotten off track, and reckon with your head trash and limiting beliefs that may hold you back from expansion and growth.

Living in congruence with your Human Design is a becoming process. It is not a quick fix or something that happens overnight. It is both a peeling back of the layers and an embracing of who you have always been. It is a journey of getting back to the true nature of who you are. Enjoy this journey and its ups and downs. Choose in each and every moment this new iteration of yourself so that you can look back in a year and say, "This is how far I've come." Choose yourself in each moment even if it doesn't always make sense. Embrace your quirks and authenticity. The world needs you to own who you are. Express your unique voice and perspective. Never settle, and be willing to challenge the status quo and the way it is always been done. You can have success in your business (and life) on your own terms. I encourage you to throw out the rules on how it has been done in your industry and say yes to how you want to do it. You've got this, and if you feel called, take the HD Your Biz pledge (on the next page).

With your design in mind,

Jamie

THE HD YOUR BIZ PLEDGE

I am honoring my strategy and authority, and I live life in high definition by leveraging my unique Human Design blueprint as a lens to guide me. I am creating a business with a strengths-aligned strategy, and I will FOCUS— Follow One Course Until Successful. I do the work of peeling back the layers of conditioning that my past lived experiences have put on me. I am becoming more and more of who I am with each passing day. I stand tall and shine my light confidently as I go about my days. I live in congruence with my purpose. If I can imagine it, I can achieve it. I am consciously creating the life I desire by honoring my inner truth. I confidently embrace the darkness of the not-self themes in my life knowing they are not mine to carry. I put down the weight of what I have been carrying. I break free from the boxes, labels, glass ceilings, and shoulds. I dance with the ebbs and flows of life's demands and boldly step into the light of who I am. I leverage my design as a lighthouse calling me home again and again when I have lost my way. I find strength in knowing the energy that I bring to the table. I share my uniqueness with the world as it is a gift to be treasured. The ripple effect of these gifts spreads far beyond what I can see. I am committed to being the author of my life. I am living life (and biz) in high definition using my unique Human Design blueprint. I pledge to revamp, revise, recondition, and reiterate as many times as necessary in order to become and live in congruence with the truest, highest, and best version of myself. I am living life in high definition.

ABOUT THE AUTHOR

J amie is a Human Design expert with a difference. With a unique ability to take a hawk-eye view and her fearless need to explore the depths and evolve, Jamie is on a mission to innovate and liberate you from false beliefs and obstacles that hold you back in your life and biz.

Starting in business in her twenties, Jamie has cultivated a diverse ecosystem of knowledge and expertise, synthesized into the revolutionary system known as Ecocentric Human Design - which includes the following programs:

- Social Made Simple
- Productize for Profit
- Business Ecosystem Builders
- HD Your Biz
- HD in the Wild

Jamie believes that your voice is important and essential to a future where we can thrive, not only as individuals but also connected to the beauty of a sustainable ecosystem. She firmly believes that your success doesn't have to cost the earth.

When not creating Human Design programs or coaching, Jamie can be found in Newport, RI, with her kiddos and husband hanging out in nature, paddleboarding, writing, or turning her backyard into an edible landscape.

Jamie's passions have led her in many directions. All of this has led her to appreciate sustainability on many levels and embrace the philosophy of doing more with less.

If you are ready to free your voice and create impact, Jamie can steward you to fulfillment.

RESOURCES & ADDITIONAL SUPPORT FOR DIGGING DEEPER WITH HUMAN DESIGN & BUSINESS

The HD Your Biz Show **podcast**—My weekly podcast diving into all things Human Design, business, and living life in high definition.

The blog—My blog is a great place to dive deeper into different aspects of Human Design.

The Impact Sphere—A community for people who want to live life and business in high definition using their Human Design.

HD Your Biz Workbook—I highly recommend downloading the *HD Your Biz Workbook*. In this workbook, you will find additional resources, meditations, and prompts to support you in creating a plan for leveraging your Human Design in business: www.humandesignforbusinessbook.com.

HD Snapshots—The Audio Experience—Do you want a custom private podcast feed with all aspects of your chart on it? HD Snapshot—The Audio Experience is a deep dive into your type, profile, centers, definition, authority, gates, and channels: www.hdsnapshot.com.

Business Design With Human Design—If you want to learn how to create an offer in congruence with your Human Design, this course is a great way to know which aspects of your design to look at. We dive into centers, variables, circuitry, and more when deciding what elements to include in your offer, your transformation promise, and how you attract clients: www.businessdesignwithhumandesign.com.

HD Your Biz—The 13 Week Program to HD Your Business and Life. If you want to dig deeper into strategy, branding, marketing, sales, storytelling, productivity, tech, and leadership by design, I invite you to join me on this journey: www.hdyourbiz.com.

HD Wild—If you want to incorporate Human Design into your existing expertise while getting support for your business, this is the program for you. This is a one-year, high-touch program to learn Human Design, develop your own intellectual property with this tool, and get support for living your design. I invite you to dive into the wild world of Human Design with me: www.hdinthewild.com.

HUMAN DESIGN TERMINOLOGY

Authority—Authority is the decision-making process within your unique Human Design blueprint. When you honor your decision-making process in congruence with your profile and type, you will find more congruence with your Human Design.

Centers—The foundation of Human Design information. They determine your type, profile, and strategy. Centers determine the flow of energy within your Human Design blueprint.

Conditioning—The pressure, expectation, and influence from family, friends, society, and modern culture to be something we are not. The pressure to conform to what others expect of us. The taking on of habits and strategies that repress our true self and push us out of congruence with our purpose in life.

Conscious—The black elements that appear on your chart are known as your conscious personality. You are aware of these elements to a degree and have some control over them.

Defined Centers—The colored-in aspects of your chart. In these areas, you have a set or fixed personality, and it is punctuated by the gates and channels you have coming off of the defined centers. Over time, you will only become more of who you are already. For example, if you crave consistency, you will only crave consistency more over time. This is how your unique personality shows up in the world. You have the theme; it is a matter of having access to it or lacking capacity to access it. The defined centers manifest in duality. Learning to explore and play with the polarity becomes the goal.

Definition—There are five types of definition. Definition defines how the energy flows within the different centers in your chart. The type of our definition defines whether we will have access to the continuous flow of energy within our chart. Our definition also determines how we best interact with others. This is helpful when you are building a team (or in relationships); you will want people who are complementary and who will help you bridge the definition in your design. For example, if you are a triple split definition, you will want someone to help you transform your energy into a single or split definition.

No Definition—No centers defined within the chart (Reflectors).

Single Definition—All defined channels and centers in the Human Design are connected in one continuous stream.

Simple Split Definition—There are two separate areas of definition within the chart that are not connected to one another.

Triple Split Definition—There are three separate areas of definition within the chart that are not connected to one another.

Quadruple Split Definition—There are four separate areas of definition within the chart that are not connected to one another.

Gates & Channels—The life forces (tribal, collective, and individual) that make up the intricacies of who we are and how we interact, share, support, and empower others in the world.

Incarnation Cross—This is the guiding light for your purpose in the world when you are living out your unique Human Design blueprint in an authentic and congruent way.

Intrapersonal—Lines 1, 2, 3 in the Human Design System, which are concerned with their own personal destiny. The intrapersonal lines do not need others in order to live out their purpose.

Lines—There are six lines within the Human Design System. These six lines give personality to the different types. The lines are how you learn and how you experience the world. They give color to who you are and how you go about living.

Not-Self—A clear indication that you are out of congruence with or in congruence with your design. Your mind has taken over and/or you are acting out of your conditioning.

Not-Self Themes—An indication or signal that a decision was made through the mind instead of through your strategy, typically resulting in resistance (i.e., you are out of congruence with your strategy).

Manifestors—**anger** when they have failed to inform the key parties in their life.

Projectors—**bitterness and resentment** when they have initiated and invited themselves to give advice.

Generators—**frustration** when they have initiated action without responding.

Manifesting Generators—**frustration and anger** when they have initiated action without responding and have not informed the key parties of their actions.

Profiles—There are twelve profiles within the Human Design System. Profiles are made up of two different lines—one conscious and one subconscious. The profile is how you will learn as you go about life and the personality that you bring and show to the world. In keeping with the lighthouse metaphor, you can think of the profile as the color and design that makes up your own lighthouse.

Signature Goal—The desired outcome for each of the types. This is the state achieved when the person is living in congruence with their design. It dispels the not-self and welcomes others into their ecosystem within the framework or guardrails of the strategy and authority.

Strategy—For each type within the Human Design System, there is a strategy. This strategy is the guiding principle with which they interact with the world. For example, the Projector's strategy is to wait for the invitation and recognition. Projectors will find themselves bitter if they are offering up advice without being invited in and/or recognized. Manifestors who initiate without informing can often leave people wondering what happens when they fail to inform, which is a big part of being a healthy Manifestor.

Manifestor—Initiate and inform

Generator—Know thyself and respond

Projector—Wait for the invitation (recognized or asked)

Manifesting Generator—Visualize and inform

Reflector—Wait twenty-eight days

Transpersonal—Lines 4, 5, 6 in the Human Design System who need others in order to fulfill their purpose. With a line 4, 5, or 6, one cannot live out their purpose without the other.

Type—There are five types in the Human Design System. Each type determines the overarching theme for your life and ideal strategy for how you show up in the world. The five types are Projector, Generator, Manifesting Generator, Manifestor, and Reflector. When we live our type in conjunction with our profile, we find purpose and joy.

Unconscious—The red elements that appear on your chart are known as the unconscious personality. These are aspects of your personality that are consistent, but you may not be aware of them, nor do you have control over them. As you age, they typically become more of these parts of yourself. The red elements are pulled three months prior to your birth during a big growth spurt in the brain.

Undefined Centers—Fluid aspects within yourself that are open to receive and take on the energy of others and are subject to conditioning. Undefined centers are like filters that take in information as you go about your experience in the world. The gates on undefined centers act as anchors to shine a light on the energy that is yours inside the undefined center.

A free ebook edition is available with the purchase of this book.

To claim your free ebook edition:

1. Visit MorganJamesBOGO.com
2. Sign your name CLEARLY in the space
3. Complete the form and submit a photo of the entire copyright page
4. You or your friend can download the ebook to your preferred device

Print & Digital Together Forever.

Snap a photo   Free ebook   Read anywhere

Printed in the USA
CPSIA information can be obtained
at www.ICGtesting.com
JSHW020924130624
64551JS00005BA/316